MW00794935

Burl Ives and Keir Dullea in a scene from the New York production of "Dr. Cook's Garden."

DR. COOK'S GARDEN

BY IRA LEVIN

★

DRAMATISTS
PLAY SERVICE
INC.

DR. COOK'S GARDEN was first presented by Saint Subber at the Belasco Theatre, in New York City, on September 25, 1967. It was directed by Mr. Levin; the set and lighting were by David Hays; and the costumes by Noel Taylor. The Associate Producers were Frank Prince and Manuel Seff. The cast, in order of appearance, was as follows:

DR. JIM TENNYSON .... Keir Dullea

BEA SCHMIDT .... Bette Henritze

DORA LUDLOW .... Lee Sanders

ELIAS HART .... Bob Berger

DR. LEONARD COOK .... Burl Ives

3

CHARACTERS

Dr. Jim Tennyson

Bea Schmidt

Dora Ludlow

Elias Hart

Dr. Leonard Cook

This action takes place in the home and office of Dr. Leonard Cook, in the village of Greenfield Center, Vermont.
The time is a Friday in the fall of 1966.

ACT I—Late Afternoon

ACT II—Ten Minutes Later

ACT III—Half an Hour Later

NOTE: What in Vermont is called a town is in other states a township; an area roughly six miles square containing several separate communities. Greenfield Center, the village in which the play is set, is in Greenfield Town, which also encompasses the village of South Greenfield ("South Green") and Hart Mills; and that is what the characters mean by the word "town"—the three villages and the farms surrounding them.

5

SETTING

Dr. Cook, a bachelor, lives in a small, old, comfortable, two-story house, the ground floor of which he has given over almost entirely to his medical practice.

At the center of the stage, and occupying most of it, is his office, originally the house's living room. There are a rolltop desk and a swivel chair, a sagging davenport, another chair or two, a small table, file cabinets, and bookcases full of medical books. D. R., closed sliding doors to an inner examining room, originally the dining room. Certificates on the walls, and a framed cover of *Flower and Garden* magazine. Perhaps a fireplace or stove.

At L. the front door of the house and a small foyer, with a hall-way U. to the kitchen area. Between the foyer and the office, the lower part of the enclosed winding stairway to the second floor.

Also at L., part of the waiting room, and a reception desk.

The office is orderly but holds several decades' accumulation of records and journals. The general effect is one of comfort and old-fashioned dependability.

DR. COOK'S GARDEN

ACT I

AT RISE: *Dr. Jim Jennyson, a likeable-looking young man in a topcoat, is hugging Bea Schmidt, a middle-aged woman wearing a sweater over a white uniform. They are in the office near the foyer. Late-afternoon sunlight pours through the L. window, shafting horizontally across the office. A suitcase stands by the front door. Dora Ludlow, an elderly woman in a house-dress, hurries in from the kitchen.*

JIM. You haven't changed a bit! Not a hair, Bea! You look exactly the same!

BEA. Look at you! Just look at you! I wouldn't have known you! I swear I wouldn't have!

DORA. Jim? Is he here? Jim?

JIM. Dora!

DORA. Oh my land.

BEA. Look at him! *(Jim relinquishes Bea and hugs Dora. Bea digs in her pocket, teary-eyed.)*

DORA. What a big tall handsome man you are.

JIM. Dora! Oh, it's so good to see you again!

BEA. Oh, I never saw such a change in a person . . .

(Elias Hart, a middle aged man in work clothes, enters, L. and comes through the waiting room.)

DORA. Wait till Doc sees you! He's just going to pop with pride!

JIM. Is he in?

BEA. *(Wiping her eyes with a handkerchief.)* He's in South Green. Oh, and he wanted to be here!

JIM. The plane was early into Burlington, so I got the one o'clock bus. What are you crying for?

BEA. I can't help it!

JIM. Elias!

ELIAS. Hello, Jim. I saw you crossing the road.

7

JIM. (*Going to him and taking his hand.*) How are you?

ELIAS. Fine, thanks.

JIM. Congratulations! Doc wrote me!

DORA. I'm going to cry too.   ELIAS. Oh, it's nothing important.

JIM. What do you mean? Town constable is tremendously important! You're the force of law and order, aren't you?

ELIAS. Say, we have to call *you* Doc now too. He's Doc now
too.

JIM. Don't you dare! Doc is Doc. I'm Jim, that's all.

ELIAS. A bigger and finer-looking Jim than set out from here,
that's for sure.

JIM. (*Looks about, at Elias smiling, at Bea and Dora wiping their
eyes.*) Well. It's a pleasure to be back in Vermont, where everyone is so cold and unemotional.   (*They all smile. Bea and Dora
pocket their handkerchiefs.*)

BEA. Take your coat off.

ELIAS. How long are you here for?

JIM. Just the weekend.

BEA and DORA. Ahh, no . . .

JIM. I have to be back in Chicago Tuesday morning. (*Bea takes
his coat.*)

DORA. There's a party for you tomorrow night.

JIM. I know.

BEA. Ray and Jean Higley.

JIM. I know. I stopped off at the cemetery and Essie Bullit was
there; she told me all about it.

DORA. (*Taking the coat from Bea.*) Here, I'll hang it up. Would
you like some coffee?

JIM. I'd love some.

DORA. Bea? Elias?

BEA. Yes. Please.

ELIAS. None for me, thanks. I'm in the middle of moving some
azaleas. I have to go right out again. (*Dora goes into the foyer.*)

JIM. I'm surprised that you're still gardening.

ELIAS. Only for Doc, none of the others. Whenever I have an
hour or two I stop by. We're getting to be famous; look at that
Flower and Garden there. (*Dora, having hung Jim's coat on a
rack by the front door, exits to the kitchen.*)

JIM. Doc sent me a copy when it came out. It's great.

8

ELIAS. *Vermont Life* took some pictures too, but they haven't used them yet.

BEA. People have been coming just to see. We had a whole group from Fitchburg, Mass.

JIM. Really? (*Moves* L., *looking out the window.*)

ELIAS. Now it's nothing. You should have been here last month; pompoms and crocuses all around behind the birches there . . .

JIM. I wish I *could* have been here.

ELIAS. (*Moving to the rear door.*) I'll see you later, all right?

JIM. Right. How's *Mrs.* Hart?

ELIAS. Fine. She ran into Earl Booth's delivery truck last winter, but Doc fixed her up good as new. Better than Rudy fixed the Jeep, anyway. (*He exits. Jim and Bea smile at each other.*)

JIM. How's *your* family?

BEA. Fine. You'll see them all tomorrow night. May is pregnant.

JIM. Wonderful! When is she due?

BEA. In January.

JIM. That's great! (*He moves back toward the* C. *of the office. Bea follows along.*)

BEA. Was it as hard as they say it is, your internship?

JIM. Mmm, no, not really. I'm glad it's over with, though. (*Looks about.*) Oh, it's really something to be here again, and to look at Doc's books—which always seemed to me to be about on a par with the sacred secret tablets of God—to look at them and to think, "Glory be, I know what's in them!" When I left, all I knew was where the naked women were. (*Goes and puts his finger on the right books.*) There's one in here, on page two-hundred-and-something . . . and there's a *great* one in here. Has her legs WI-I-I-I-IDE open!

BEA. You've been in Chicago, all right.

JIM. That was right back here in little old Greenfield Center. Behind all the gee-Doc-can-I-carry-your-bag-for-you. I was really Dirty Jimmy, the young picture-looker-atter.

BEA. You sure fooled me.

JIM. Say, that elementary school is *beautiful!*

BEA. You saw it?

JIM. You can't very well miss it. Good Lord! Davistown **must be** green with envy. Was somebody being sarcastic, naming it for Lloyd Zachary?

9

BEA. No, that was Doc's idea. (*The telephone rings. Bea goes to reception desk.*) He said we should forgive the old buzzard.

JIM. Leave it to Doc.

BEA. Dr. Cook's. (*Dora enters* U. L. *with three mugs of coffee. Jim goes to take one.*)

JIM. Hey, those yellow mugs.
DORA. The last three. I put in cream and sugar; is that okay?
JIM. Perfect.

BEA. Hi, Helen. Oh, *good*. I will; he'll be glad to hear it. Yes, I think you should. At least till tomorrow.

(*Dora brings a mug to Bea.*)

BEA. He's here now. He's six-foot-two and so handsome you could die. (*Jim shies and winces.*) I will, dear. Good-by. (*Hangs up.*) Helen Scoville says you're to drop by.

JIM. I'm six-foot-one.

DORA. (*Sitting* R. *with her mug.*) How's Pete?

BEA. All better.

DORA. Thank the Lord.

JIM. What was wrong with him?

BEA. A stomach ache, but Doc was afraid it might be hepatitis.

DORA. Thank the good Lord it's not. (*Jim sits, they all sip their coffee.*)

JIM. Well? Who's married and who's dead?

DORA. Oh, where to begin, where to begin . . .

BEA. You know about Fran Scudder and Bobby Arvold . . .

JIM. Mm-hmm.

DORA. Alice Hart and Roy Bullit?

JIM. Married or dead?

DORA. Married! They've got two little girls already!

JIM. My God, they *hated* each other!

BEA. Carol Zachary and Ab Sanford—

JIM. No.

DORA. And *Jean* Sanford and Charley Rausch—

JIM. No!

DORA. Oh, yes.   BEA. That's right.

JIM. What happened to Barbara Barnum?

DORA. Moved away to New York.   BEA. She went to New York.

JIM. And Barbara Rousseau? (*A pause.*)

BEA. She's married to Perry Booth. They had a little girl that was

10

—mentally retarded, but she died. The summer before last. Now Barbara's pregnant again, and worried to death, poor thing.

DORA. Dick Scudder is in Washington, in the Health, Education, and Welfare Department.

JIM. Great.

DORA. The Lick boys and George Rousseau are in Vietnam.

BEA. And Ray Allbright.

JIM. That many?

DORA. Jim Rausch is a prisoner.

JIM. Oh God.

BEA. And who's dead: there's—

DORA. Darryl Maxim—

BEA. Yes, and—   JIM. Who? Darryl who?

DORA. Darryl Maxim; the constable before Elias.

JIM. I didn't know him. Ted Ruth senior was constable when I left.

DORA. And *he* died and then it was Darryl Maxim.

BEA. From Hart Mills.

DORA. Lloyd Zachary's dead and got the new school named for him.

JIM. I know; I thought I was seeing things.

BEA. George Suggs.

JIM. Old Man Beecher must be gone.

BEA. No, he isn't; he's a hundred and eight years old!

DORA. And walks as smart as a rooster—at least when he knows you're watching him.

BEA. The births and the moving-ins have kept ahead of the deaths and the moving-aways, and we're up to fourteen hundred and forty-four.

DORA. Forty-five when Mrs. John Forrest has her baby. She's a week late.

JIM. And still the same contentment everywhere. I felt it the minute I stepped off the bus.

DORA. We're blessed, although what we've done to deserve it is more than J can see.

BEA. I was talking to Ruth Scudder the other day and she said that Ann Fletcher is— (*Dr. Leonard Cook enters* L. *He is near seventy, energetic and pre-occupied, wearing a car coat over a wool shirt and taking off a peaked cap. He is almost at his desk before he becomes aware of the women and Jim. Jim smiles. Doc*

11

stares at him, automatically putting his bag on the corner of the desk.)

DOC. Jimmy . . . !

JIM. Hello, Doc. *(Doc smiles, then beams. He goes to Jim, looks him up and down, and takes his outstretched hand with a joy beyond words. He pokes Jim's shoulder and then, overwhelmed, embraces him. Dora rises. Doc draws back and looks again at Jim, shaking his head marvelingly.)*

DOC. My God, my God!

JIM. The plane was early, so I got the one o'clock bus.

DOC. *(To Dora.)* Will you look at him?

JIM. Look at you; you look wonderful.

DOC. *(Taking off his coat.)* Dr. Tennyson!

JIM. *(Smiling, bowing his head.)* At your service, Dr. Cook.

BEA. We're having a coffee clatch.

DORA. *(Reaching for Doc's cap and coat.)* Would you like a cup?

DOC. No, I had some with Jack Brenner. Oh thanks, thank you, Dora.

JIM. They're filling me in on all the vital statistics. *(Dora goes to the foyer coat rack. Doc takes another look at Jim.)*

DOC. Your mother would have been so proud of you, Jimmy. And your father too, of course; he would have been too. How long are you staying?

JIM. I have to be in Chicago Tuesday morning.

DOC. Tuesday? Why, that's no visit, just a weekend; how are you going to see everybody? You stay longer, stay the week!

JIM. I wish I could, Doc, but I can't.

DOC. Did they tell you about the party tomorrow night? *(Jim nods.)* And Mary Broom and the Reverend want you for Sunday dinner.

DORA. *(Taking Jim's mug.)* You won't know the inside of the church; carpet, new pews; was the new organ while you were here?

JIM. Sure it was.

DOC. *(To Bea.)* How many are waiting? *(Dora takes Bea's mug.)*

BEA. Not a one. I put everybody off till tomorrow and Monday, so you could be free for Jim.

DOC. Good. That's wonderful. (*To Dora.*) You made up the bed, didn't you?

DORA. Yes, and I'm setting the table too. The *table*, not the desk. (*To Jim.*) You see that he feeds you at the table tonight.

JIM. I'll do what I can.

DORA. Tomorrow morning I want to see *spots* on the tablecloth. (*Exits to the kitchen.*)

BEA. Helen Scoville just called.

DOC. She did?

BEA. Pete's stomach ache is completely gone.

DOC. That's a relief. (*To Jim.*) It looked a little like hepatitis. With the one central school that could be terrible.

JIM. At least the old schools kept us in three separate bunches.

BEA. That's the only good thing you can say for them.

DOC. (*Taking a long printed form from his desk.*) What's this, Bea?

BEA. I filled it in; you just have to sign.

DOC. (*Looking it over.*) Damn insurance companies . . .

JIM. I *saw* the school; it's beautiful.

DOC. (*Taking out his pen and signing the form.*) It's worth all the fights and maneuvering. I'll show you the inside of it tomorrow. (*Giving the form to Bea.*) Mary Ann Forrest didn't call?

BEA. No.

DOC. (*Sitting at the desk.*) I'll be with you in one minute, Jim. I just want to get my notes down while they're fresh in my mind.

JIM. Sure, go ahead.

DOC. Put these over there, will you? (*He gives Jim two or three 5x7 file cards.*)

JIM. Sure.

BEA. (*About to go out, turns.*) I'll file them.

JIM. It's all right, I remember the system. (*Doc takes another card from a file drawer; Bea goes into the waiting room; Jim begins filing the cards. Doc writes; Bea, sitting at the reception desk, folds the form and puts it into an envelope; Jim files.*)

DOC. (*While he writes.*) Always get your notes down the first chance you get. The next chance may not come until God-knows-when.

JIM. (*Smiles tolerantly at him.*) That's good advice, Doc. (*Doc replaces the card, selects another one, and writes more. Jim speaks softly.*) Shall I bring in some firewood for you?

13

DOC. No, you go on home now, Jimmy. Your mother's going to give me holy hell as it is. (*Doc goes on writing, Jim grins, and then Doc realizes he's been had. He covers his eyes and groans, then laughs with Jim.*) I walked into that one all right, didn't I?

JIM. You sure did.

DOC. You're a tricky young fellow!

JIM. You're an easy fellow to trick!

DOC. I'm almost done now.

JIM. That's all right, go ahead. It's nice to look at everything again. (*Doc resumes writing. Jim browses, looks toward* L. *window.*) That's not bad, having the town constable for your gardener.

DOC. Is he here now?

JIM. Yes.

DOC. (*Finished, re-filing the last card and closing his pen.*) Good; I've got a sack of Darwin tulips that should have gone in days ago. Is that what he's doing, planting bulbs?

JIM. He's transplanting azaleas.

DOC. (*Rising, going* L.) I hope he puts the bulbs in . . . (*Jim steps back, Doc goes to the window and looks out.*) Mm, yes, I can see where—good. Yes, before I put him up to the other selectmen—(*Turning to Jim.*)—I made him promise that come what may he'd go right on taking care of the garden. Green all ten fingers, that's what Elias has. (*Pointing at the* Flower and Garden *cover as he goes back to the desk.*) That cover is his doing, not mine.

JIM. You're the one who plans everything.

DOC. (*Sitting, calling.*) Bea! Go on home!

BEA. (*Looking up from writing, calling back.*) And help with the cooking? No, thanks, five on the dot is when I leave! (*Doc swivels to face Jim. They exchange smiles.*)

DOC. Jim, Jimmy, Jimmy!

JIM. Hi, Doc.

DOC. It's about time you kept your word, you ungrateful son of a gun.

JIM. Every summer I planned to come and every summer there was a chance to earn some money or get half a year ahead. And then *after* school—

DOC. That's all right, that's all right. I know.

14

DOC. I know, I know. I'm glad you're here now. You can't pos-
sibly stay the week?

JIM. No, I can't. I wish I could; I'd forgotten what it's like here,
how peaceful and serene everything is.

DOC. It's not completely idyllic, don't kid yourself. We had a
terrible brush fire in South Green two weeks ago.

JIM. Mmm. In Chicago they've got things called "crime" and
"violence" that—well, you wouldn't believe me if I told you.

DOC. (*A smile and a moment of silence.*) You're all ready to set
up shop?

JIM. Mm-hmm.

DOC. And you're definitely not going to specialize.

JIM. Definitely not.

DOC. It's a shame; a boy as good-looking as you could make a
fortune in gynecology. Where do you stand with the draft?

JIM. I'm not sure; that's why I have to be in Chicago Tuesday
morning. I've asked to be reclassified 4F because of my arm.

DOC. Has it been giving you any trouble?

JIM. No, it hasn't. I'm not completely convinced that we belong
there—in Vietnam. That we're going to stop Communism or that
we should even *try* to stop it by dropping bombs and shedding
blood.

DOC. You would be doctoring, not dropping bombs.

JIM. I'd be cooperating, though, doing my bit to help . . . (*He
sits on the davenport and thinks; Doc watches him.*)

DOC. Do you want my old X-rays of your arm? Or a letter
from me?

JIM. No, Doc, I came here to visit; I didn't come to get anything.
The doctors at the hospital gave me enough X-rays to paper a
room with.

DOC. (*Rising.*) Take the original ones too; it's a good idea. I
know the way draft boards think; I'm on one, don't forget.
(*Looks over a dozen accordion files stacked on bookshelves in an
out-of-the-way corner.*)

JIM. I honestly don't think that it's necessary, Doc.

DOC. I've got enough of my boys getting shot at over there. Both
of the Lick boys, Ray Allbright; Jim Rausch has been taken
prisoner. There it is, R through Z. Can you reach this file for
me?

JIM. (*Hopping up.*) Sure thing.

15

DOC. The one in the corner, R through Z. (*Jim gets it.*) I *think* they're in here. Thank you. Mmh! (*That at the sight of dust. He blows it from the top of the file. Jim brushes his hands. Doc puts the file on the nearest convenient resting place and unties it.*) Where are you going to practice? Have you decided?

JIM. No, that's something else that's up in the air. After Tuesday, if I get the reclassification, I'll make up my mind. There's a girl who might have a say in the question too.

DOC. (*Looking up.*) Is there?

JIM. (*Nodding.*) We're about ready to take the plunge. This weekend apart is to help us make up our minds.

DOC. That's wonderful news!

JIM. (*Taking out his wallet.*) Her name is Elizabeth Rodseth. She works at WBKB, a television station. (*Doc brushes his hands and takes the snapshot Jim offers.*)

DOC. Oh, isn't she lovely! Isn't she a lovely looking girl! Is she an actress?

JIM. No, no; she does research for a news show. I knew her at Northwestern.

DOC. (*Returning the snapshot.*) She's beautiful; don't you let her get away.

JIM. That's what she says. (*Gets lost in the snapshot.*)

DOC. (*Waits, smiles, cues him.*) And you haven't decided where you would settle . . .

JIM. I'm for staying right in Chicago, but Liz wants to get back to small-town life. She's from a place in Michigan that's even smaller than Greenfield. (*He puts the snapshot back in his wallet. Doc resumes looking through the file.*) I'd hate having to drive as far to a hospital as you do, though, and I want plenty of other doctors around, for consultations and just to talk with. (*Puts away his wallet.*)

DOC. Here they are. (*He draws two X-ray pictures from the file, glances at them against the light, and passes them to Jim. Jim holds one up, looks at it, and draws breath hissingly between his teeth.*)

JIM. Ooh! Poor little me. Whew! That bastard really clobbered me, didn't he. (*Looks at the second picture.*) It's funny to think I'm holding it with the same arm. Funny, hell; it's miraculous.

DOC. You were young.

JIM. I had a good doctor.

DOC. (*Smiling, gesturing for the pictures.*) I'll put them in an envelope. (*Jim gives Doc the pictures, Doc takes them to the desk, rummages among the papers there.*)

JIM. Shall I put this back on the shelf?

DOC. Would you, please?

JIM. Sure.

DOC. I felt the same way you do when I first came here.

JIM. (*Tying the file.*) Then why did you come?

DOC. For a very good reason. I was starving. It was the middle of the Depression and doctors in the cities weren't making a nickel a week. Not the young ones, anyway. (*He finds an envelope and begins putting the picture into it. Jim returns the file to its place on the shelf.*) Greenfield had an ad in the *Journal*, and I figured that country people would at least pay with food if they couldn't pay with cash.

JIM. You were right about that.

DOC. I didn't look forward to being the only doctor, but after a while my feelings changed, and yours would too, Jimmy. I'd fight like hell now if someone else wanted to come near. (*Gives Jim the closed envelope.*) Having a whole town in your care is completely different from being a city doctor. You know each and every person in the place, know them better than anyone else does—

JIM. Better than the Reverend?

DOC. Sure, better than the Reverend! He knows the women, some of the kids; the men don't open up to him the way they do to me. He doesn't know *me*, but I know *him*. He's scared to death he's—well, I mustn't say. In the city your patients are—disconnected. You've got a man but not his wife, somebody else's friend, another man's sweetheart. All separate. But in a town like this, a one-doctor town, you've got them all—the wife, the husband, the friend; the sweethearts, the children—all of them tied together, all *involved* with each other. So *you* get involved. You find that you can't take vacations, because every day's a day one of them wants you, and that one is connected to six others, and those six connected to six *times* six.

JIM. It sounds even worse than I thought it was.

DOC. There are *rewards*, Jimmy, wonderful rewards! Looking into a classroom full of kids—a *greenhouse* full of opening flowers!—and you're the one who delivered every last one of them!

17

And delivered most of their mothers and fathers too! Keeping up with what's new because you don't have specialists handy to lean on; studying, and knowing you're ahead of most other doctors. Preserving an Old Man Beecher—he's sound as a bell, would you believe it? Spotting a Dick Scudder, a Jim Tennyson, a Eunice Wilcox; seeing that they're encouraged, given room to spread and blossom . . . (*A thought checks him.*) well, maybe it's not for you; you've got a girl and you'll have a family. Find your own answer, Chicago or someplace in-between size; don't be swayed by me. I hated all cities, if you want the truth. The noise and the people close around made me jumpy as a cat. (*The telephone rings. Bea answers it and Doc goes quickly to his desk.*)
BEA. Dr. Cook's. Is it anything urgent? Because if it—
DOC. Hello? Yes. Who's this? (*Bea hangs up with an air of "I tried."*) Oh? Hm, that doesn't sound like Frank at all. Have you got him in bed? (*He opens a file drawer, finds, takes out, and scans a card, listening as he does so. Jim watches him.*) No, I don't think it would be that. Just a minute. (*Covers the mouthpiece.*) You want to unpack, don't you; make some phone calls?
JIM. Yes.
DOC. (*Into the phone again.*) Sharon? It's quiet here now, so I'll come over and take a look at him. (*Bea rises and comes to the waiting room doorway.*) Of course it isn't. I'll be there in ten minutes. (*Hangs up, puts down the card.*) Frank Prugo. Hasn't been sick a day since June, 1939, when he had the measles. Threw up and has a-hundred-point-four.
JIM. Flu?
DOC. Maybe. (*Going to the coat rack.*) You make your phone calls. I'll be back in half an hour.
JIM. You know, Doc, there's one new thing in medicine that you haven't kept up with.
DOC. (*Getting into his coat.*) What's that?
JIM. It's called Not Making So Many House Calls.
BEA. I've been telling him about that for fifteen years.
JIM. It works wonders. The doctor gains weight, his color improves . . .
DOC. (*At the desk again, picking up his bag.*) While I'm on my way I'll think of something funny to say back to you. See you tomorrow, Bea.
BEA. Good night.

DOC. Tell her about your girl friend—Bob Hope. (*He goes out. Jim takes out his wallet. Bea goes to him.*)

JIM. Her name is Elizabeth Rodseth—

BEA. And she's from a small town in Michigan; I know. Let me see.

JIM. Did you ever think of just cutting a little peephole? (*Gives her the snapshot.*)

BEA. Oh, isn't she a beautiful girl! Congratulations.

JIM. Don't rush me. (*Takes the snapshot and puts it back in his wallet.*)

BEA. Will you bring her here so we can meet her?

JIM. If we—

BEA. I'll bet she'd like it here!

JIM. (*Looking about, pocketing his wallet.*) Yes, she would. I know she would.

BEA. (*A suppressed tension becoming evident.*) Are you *sure* you don't want to live in a small town again? In *this* town?

JIM. What's wrong, Bea?

BEA. Doc isn't well. I think he's had a heart attack. (*They are motionless for a moment.*)

JIM. When?

BEA. In August. He stayed in his room all one morning—said he was catching up on magazines—and when he came down in the afternoon he was gray, and so tired looking. That's why I wrote you and reminded you to come see us. He'll let *you* examine him, I'll bet, but he won't go *near* the new doctor in Davistown or Nat Crumley in Hardwick.

JIM. I'll do an EKG on him this evening.

BEA. Don't you let him talk you out of it.

JIM. I'll tie him down if I have to.

BEA. Good!

JIM. But if it *was* a coronary, Bea, all I can do is tell him to take it easy. You know how much good *that's* going to do.

BEA. He would take it easy if—you came in and shared the practice with him, and eventually took it over . . .

JIM. (*Shakes his head.*) He doesn't want that. It's his town. He just said it; he'd fight if any other doctor tried to move in.

BEA. Not *you*. You're almost his son. He'd love to have you!

JIM. I'm not so sure. He'd have dropped a hint just now, or come right out and asked me. And it wouldn't be right; two doctors here, when there are towns around with none at all. I'll talk to him. Maybe I can get him to say no to a couple of his midnight calls. Even if it wasn't a coronary. It may not have been, you know.

BEA. I've been worrying about him so. (*She turns a light on, for the room has grown shadowed.*) I think of poor Darryl Maxim, who was young and in perfect health, and then I think of Doc. He's near seventy, Jim, and has this whole town on his shoulders!

JIM. He's a naturalized Vermonter by now; he'll live longer than Old Man Beecher, so stop worrying. Is that what Darryl Maxim died of, a coronary?

BEA. (*Nods.*) Thirty-two years old.

JIM. Mmh. He must have had *something* wrong with him.

BEA. Nothing.

JIM. Really?

BEA. Look for yourself. So I can't stop worrying about a man twice as old who works twice as hard. Now listen, don't you get me in dutch with Doc. (*Jim goes to a file drawer—not one that Doc looked into earlier—and opens it.*) You make out as if I didn't say anything about anything, and taking an EKG is your own idea—because he doesn't look right to you.

JIM. (*Flicking through the file cards.*) Okay.

BEA. I'd better check the ink and paper. (*Goes U. and opens one of the sliding doors partway.*) Do you think you can cope with our old antique? (*She slips into the examining room and turns the light on. Jim draws a card from the file. An anatomy chart and the end of an examining table can be seen through the door.*)

JIM. The new ones aren't that different . . .

BEA. (*Calling from within.*) I'm going to lay out the electrodes for you!

JIM. (*Comes D., studying the card, and after a moment calls to Bea.*) What does R stand for?

BEA. (*Off.*) What?

JIM. (*Louder.*) What does R stand for?

BEA. (*Comes to the door.*) R?

JIM. On Darryl Maxim's card. On the line before where the coronary is entered. (*Bea comes D.; Jim shows her the card.*)

BEA. I don't know. Doc has all his little symbols and abbreviations . . . the G's and the B are for Darryl's children, two girls

20

and a boy. I don't know what the R is. You see how clean his card is?

JIM. You were right. (*Going back to the open file.*) I thought he might have had something in his childhood that affected his heart. It's funny he didn't.

BEA. (*Going back u. to the door.*) I laid out the electrodes but I didn't plug them in. So it wouldn't look too prepared in advance. (*Reaching in, she turns the light off in the examining room. Jim, still holding Darryl Maxim's card, is lifting out other cards, glancing at them, and tucking them back into the file. Bea closes the examining-room door.*) I wish you'd think more about what I said, Jim; about coming in with Doc.

JIM. Here's another one with an R on it. Hannah Meserve.

BEA. Oh what a sour old woman that was. Sour and selfish. You wouldn't remember her, would you.

JIM. (*Studying the card, comparing it with Maxim's.*) Mm-mmn.

BEA. The joke was that she should have been named "Hannah Serve-*me*" instead of "Hannah Me-*serve.*" That was what everyone used to say. She was Essie Bullit's mother, and after her husband Howard died she moved in with Essie and Ben and made servants out of them; had them fetching and doing for her, Essie and Ben and all four kids. (*Dora enters from the kitchen, carrying her coat and a paper bag.*) She used to sit in the parlor all day long, playing bridge from a book against Ely Culbertson—this is Hannah Meserve—and all day long saying "Bring me this" and "Go and do that," slapping the children with this ivory backscratcher she had.

DORA. (*Putting her coat and the bag on a chair.*) Hannah Serve-me is what she *should* have been called, not Hannah Meserve. It's five after.

BEA. Essie never *could* say boo to her, and Ben was too kind-hearted to send her packing. He got an ulcer, he was so upset.

DORA. Her funeral was remarkable in that it was so poorly attended. (*Bea goes to the coat rack and gets her coat. Dora, sitting, directs a question to her.*) Pneumonia it was, wasn't it?

BEA. That's right.   JIM. That's right. Preceded by

R.

BEA. (*Coming back in, putting on her coat.*) Ask Doc; he'll tell you what it means. (*Jim puts the cards on the desk and helps Bea*

21

with her coat.) Thanks. I told Jim about Doc and he's going to check his heart.

DORA. And the other?

BEA. He's going to think about it. Aren't you? This is the finest little town in Vermont and you know it.

JIM. (*To Dora.*) I like Chicago.

BEA. But his girl friend likes a small town. Show her the picture.

JIM. I think it's rubbed away by now. (*Gets out the wallet and the snapshot.*)

BEA. You call me if you have any trouble with the cardiograph.

JIM. (*Giving the snapshot to Dora.*) I will.

DORA. Oh, my!

BEA. Isn't she a beauty?

DORA. But sensible looking too. She'd fit in here perfectly.

BEA. (*To Jim.*) Try to call me *after*, but don't let him hear you.

JIM. I'll try.

BEA. Good night, Dora.

DORA. (*Giving the snapshot back to Jim.*) Good night. Tell May about the baby clothes.

BEA. Clean forgot! Good night, Jim.

JIM. Good night. See you in the morning.

BEA. You'd better give Ray and Jean a call.

JIM. I'm going to. (*Bea exits L. Jim puts the snapshot away.*)

DORA. Congratulations.

JIM. Don't rush me.

DORA. You can make your call if you want. Marshall picks me up at ten after—(*Gesturing L.*)—in front of Elias's. He's working up at the asbestos mill now.

JIM. Is he?

DORA. They're running two shifts, because of the space race.

JIM. You mean asbestos from Greenfield is used in the rockets?

DORA. In the gantries; there was a big story in the *Courier*. And we're getting a little plant that's going to make transistors too, on the other side of Hart Mills on Route Fourteen.

JIM. The town is waxing wealthy.

DORA. Yes, Jim, that's right. I don't know what you'll find in Chicago that you won't find here.

JIM. Well, hospitals and other doctors, and theatres, restaurants, museums, libraries, department stores—

22

DORA. I'll tell you *one* thing you won't find there—happier people.

JIM. No, I won't; I know. I've never been anywhere else where life seemed so good and satisfying.

DORA. We're blessed. It's as simple as that. Even Davistown, Hardwick, Morrisville, they don't have the good fortune we do. Oh, I know, you were no choirboy to begin with and you're probably an all-out heathen by now, but God has smiled on this town and given it His special love and protection; I know that for a fact. The Legion picnic in 1962; three hundred and fifty of us could have perished that day—that's how many of the sandwiches there were—but we all came through with only upset stomachs, and the one who did die, the only one, was Lloyd Zachary. Now don't you think God had a hand in that someplace?

JIM. No, I don't.

DORA. We'd still have the three one-room schools if Lloyd hadn't died, and be fighting in the courts the way Davistown is. God watches this town, and when He takes, He takes for a reason. Like Hannah Meserve we were talking about, spreading unhappiness all around her.

JIM. What about Darryl Maxim?

DORA. I don't say the reason's always crystal-clear to human eyes. Darryl, your mother, Laura Scoville . . . who can say why? But more often than not you can say why; even with the little ones, where it's almost always the ones that have something wrong with them—humpbacked, like the McClure baby, or not all there, like Perry and Barbara Booth's. (*She finds a loose button on her dress and winds the thread around it. Jim watches her, motionless, held by thought.*) I had this same talk with Darryl, just a day or two before he died. He stopped by here. Right around this time of day it was.

JIM. What was wrong with him?

DORA. Nothing, he just wanted to talk to Doc. And Bea was gone and Doc was out and I was waiting for Marshall. And we talked about God's judgment on each of us—the Reverend had preached about it that Sunday in honor of Old Man Beecher's birthday. (*Jim goes back to the file.*) And Darryl said it was wonderful that nice people like Livvy Sawyer and Old Man Beecher lived to such ripe old ages . . . (*Jim takes a card out,*

23

Dora watches him.) . . . and mean people, like George Suggs who had died a few weeks before . . . is that Darryl's card?

JIM. (*Studying it.*) Lloyd Zachary's. (*Picks up the other two cards from the desk, looks at Dora.*) Go ahead, I'm listening.

DORA. Well . . . that's all. I talked with Darryl the way we're talking now.

JIM. Did *he* look at any of these cards?

DORA. No. Why should he? He wouldn't have understood them even if he had. He asked me if there'd always been—nobody seriously impaired in the town, and I said no, long ago there'd been Anne Arkham, who was blind, and Sax Rousseau and a few others, but they'd all died or been cured or moved away, like Anne did. That's all. And then Doc came back and I went out. And I'd better be going out now. (*Rises and begins putting on her coat.*)

JIM. When I came to Chicago, I was—surprised to see blind people, and mute people finger-talking, people with an arm or a leg missing; I knew they existed, of course, but I was—surprised at the sight of them . . .

DORA. It's what I said; we're blessed. Vermont is the most favored state in the Union, and we're the most favored town in Vermont. The Lord takes good care of us. (*Picks up her bag.*) Now look, that table is all set in there, so don't you let Doc eat in here. The world won't come to an end if he's not right next to the telephone; you tell him I said so.

JIM. All right.

DORA. There's lamb stew and chocolate cream pie. I hope you enjoy it.

JIM. I will.

DORA. Good night.

JIM. Good night, Dora.

DORA. (*Takes a final loving look at him.*) My, you've grown up nicely. (*She exits L. Jim stands looking after her for a moment, then moves to the desk. He turns the desk lamp on—it has grown quite dark outside—and sits down in Doc's chair. He looks at the three cards in his hand, studies them intently, takes down one of Doc's medical books. Elias enters L. and comes softly through the waiting room, he looks in.*)

ELIAS. Doc?

JIM. (*Turning.*) It's me.

24

ELIAS. Oh. I thought you were Doc, sitting there with the cards in your hand.

JIM. He's out on a call. He should be back—in a few minutes.

ELIAS. Will you give him a message for me?

JIM. Sure.

ELIAS. (*Coming into the room.*) Tell him it got dark before I could take out the yew tree but I'll come by and do it tomorrow afternoon. All right?

JIM. I'll tell him.

ELIAS. Thank you.

JIM. How do you like being constable, Elias?

ELIAS. Fine. There's nothing to it, really. When the kids have a dance I make sure there's no alcohol, and when Iz Rausch and his wife start throwing dishes I go quiet them down. Any real trouble, I call the State Police. There never is any, though.

JIM. (*Rising.*) No sin or crime in Greenfield Town.

ELIAS. Not with George Rousseau in the Army, there isn't.

JIM. And George Suggs dead.

ELIAS. Yes.

JIM. What do you do when somebody dies?

ELIAS. Do?

JIM. As constable.

ELIAS. (*Shrugs.*) Nothing. Doc makes out a certificate and gives it to Evalyn. Evalyn Ruth. She's the clerk now.

JIM. What if it's a—suspicious death?

ELIAS. Well . . . Doc is the regional medical examiner, so he would report it to the state pathologist. In Montpelier. There's never been a suspicious death though; Doc always knows what people die of.

JIM. Yes. Of course.

ELIAS. The truth is I'm getting paid for doing next to nothing. Only don't say I said so.

JIM. I won't.

ELIAS. Don't forget to tell Doc about the yew tree, because otherwise he's going to see it there in the morning and think the sticker fell off and go all the way out to put on another one.

JIM. The sticker?

ELIAS. That's how he tells me what to do, now that I don't come in on regular days any more. He has these little orange stickers—they glow, sort of—and he takes them in his pocket whenever he goes out in the garden. Anything he wants me to do, he just puts a sticker on the plant or whatever and marks it; P for prune, T for transplant, and so on. We have a whole code he worked out. That way, I can find something to do any time I come by, even if he's out, or busy with someone and can't speak to me. (*Backs* L. *to go.*) When you're through eating why don't you come over and say hello to Helen? She's looking forward to seeing you.

JIM. Maybe I will . . .

ELIAS. Try to. We've got a color television. (*He turns and goes. Jim glances at the cards in his hand and looks up again.*)

JIM. What does R stand for, Elias?

ELIAS. (*Stops and turns.*) Remove. Did you see one of the stickers on your way in? (*Jim stands motionless.*) Jim? (*Jim looks at him.*) Did you see one of the stickers on your way in?

JIM. (*Nods.*) Yes.

ELIAS. There's not a weed or a dead branch or a hurt plant that Doc doesn't notice it and see that it's put right, either by him or by me. That's what keeps the garden so perfect all the time. (*He exits* L. *Jim sits and puts a hand over his eyes. The curtain falls.*)

END OF ACT ONE

ACT II

Ten minutes later. Jim is standing at R. watching intently as Doc lets himself in at the door L. Jim has put back the cards he took from the file and closed it. His suitcase is where it was. He has been pacing and stewing.

DOC. Hi.

JIM. (*Gathers himself.*) Hello.

DOC. (*Going to the desk and putting down his bag.*) I stopped in at the Hopwoods', right across from Frank Prugo. Their baby has God-awful eczema. (*Taking off his coat.*) You were right about Frank's flu, but it's good I went anyway. Sharon looks terrible; she's lost over ten pounds in the last two months and she was underweight to begin with. I made her promise to come in Monday or Tuesday. (*On the way to the coat rack he sees the suitcase.*) Haven't you unpacked yet?

JIM. No.

DOC. (*Hanging up his coat and cap.*) Did you make your calls?

JIM. No. (*Doc turns and looks questioningly at him.*) I was talking with Bea and Dora. And Elias.

DOC. He's gone?

JIM. Yes. They're all gone. (*Doc returns to the desk.*) He said he'll come over tomorrow and—take out the yew tree. It got too dark.

DOC. (*Sitting.*) Mm.

JIM. He didn't want you to go out and put another sticker on it.

DOC. (*Looking at a slip of paper.*) Ann Zachary?

JIM. She called just a few minutes ago.

DOC. (*Picking up the phone.*) Did she say what for?

JIM. No.

DOC. (*Jiggles the crossbar.*) Zenia? Oh? What are *you* doing on the board at this hour? Oh. Ring Ann Zachary for me, will you? Thanks. (*To Jim.*) Would you turn that lamp on, please, Jim? (*Jim goes silently R.*) Hello, Ann? Yes. (*Jim turns another lamp on, then stands watching Doc, who is searching the desktop for*

27

Frank Prugo's card while he listens.) Oh sure, that's perfectly all right. Anything she wants, at this point. No, no, whatever she wants. I only meant that for the first three days. You can give her anything she asks for. Good, that's fine. I'll stop in sometime during the weekend. Good-by, dear. (*Hangs up, uncaps his pen, and begins writing on Prugo's card.*) I'll be with you in a minute. I want to get my notes down while they're fresh in my mind.

JIM. Go ahead. (*Doc writes, Jim watches him.*)

DOC. (*Exchanging cards.*) Why don't you unpack now?

JIM. I will. In a minute. (*Doc writes again. Jim moves L. a wary, watchful crossing.*) I was looking at—some of your records.

DOC. Mm?

JIM. (*Takes a deep breath.*) Some of your—abbreviations and symbols are—hard to figure out. (*An amused, self-satisfied grunt from Doc.*) What does—R stand for? (*Doc goes on writing. After a moment:*)

DOC. R?

JIM. That's right.

DOC. (*Writes more.*) It's hard to say, right off. That's one I haven't used in quite a while. I have so many of them. (*Turns farther away from Jim to file the card he was writing on.*)

JIM. You used it on Darryl Maxim's card. In July.

DOC. Did I?

JIM. And George Suggs's, not long before.

DOC. Rest. It means I told them to rest. (*Rises, smiling at Jim.*) I have so damn many of those little short cuts that I—

JIM. It's on Susanna Booth's card too. She was twenty-two months old and mentally retarded. Did you tell *her* to rest?

DOC. It means something else in relation to children. It means *repeat*—a treatment or prescription that I gave before. (*Going to Jim with a laugh, clapping him on the shoulder.*) Listen, forget about my damn records, will you? I ought to move half of 'em out to the garage and have some room in here! Listen, Jim. Listen, you go up and unpack your suitcase, okay? And I'll go in and see what Dora made for us, and we'll eat, and then—I'll share you with Ray and Jean, and Mary and the Reverend. Everyone is so anxious to see you, Jim. This town's been talking about nothing else for two whole weeks! Now you go on, okay? Go on up and unpack. (*He starts Jim L. Jim crosses from him slowly, unwillingly.*) Say, do you know what I've got? A bottle

28

of very fine wine that Earl Booth gave to Jack Brenner and Jack Brenner gave to me. Last Christmas. The only problem now is going to be finding it. (*Jim stops near the doorway to the foyer and turns around and faces Doc.*) Dora probably put it God-knows-where. I'll find it though. I can't think of a better occasion for opening it. (*Jim stands looking at him in pained indecision.*) What is it, Jim? What's wrong?

JIM. Doc . . .

DOC. Yes?

JIM. This may sound awfully crazy, but do you know what I think R stands for?

DOC. I *told* you what it stands for, Jim; rest or repeat. Now what are you going on about it for?

JIM. I think it stands for—remove. (*A pause.*)

DOC. Well it does. In the garden. But—not in here. That *does* sound crazy, Jim. Remove? Why would I put "remove" on somebody's record? You remove—*plants;* you don't remove people! Not that I wouldn't like to once in a while, believe me! (*With a laugh he moves away from Jim. Jim takes a step after him, pointing at the drug cabinet.*)

JIM. The poison on that bottom shelf; you've got more than Cokely Memorial has with six floors and an annex.

DOC. (*Turning sharply.*) Were you in that cabinet?

JIM. I looked through the glass, I read the Latin now. Doc?

DOC. (*A pause, a nod.*) Yes, I've got more poison than you'd expect. I don't get fresh supplies every day or two, the way your hospital does. I've got more bandages than you'd expect too, in the closet in there. I've got six gallons of Zephiran sitting out in the garage. This isn't the heart of Chicago; this is a little town that's snowbound more winters than not.

JIM. *Kinds* of poison, Doc. You've got things there's no reason to have.

DOC. (*A pause, then he laughs at Jim and points at him.*) You've been working too hard, that's what's going on here! Studying for your tests after a year of interning. Rest is what *you* need. R, for rest. Shall I get your card out and mark it on it? (*He laughs, Jim doesn't.*)

JIM. Doc . . . have you killed anybody?

DOC. It wouldn't surprise me; you've seen me on Saturday mornings, getting them in and out in ten seconds.

JIM. Intentionally! I mean intentionally.

DOC. No, Jim. No, I haven't. I haven't "removed" anybody. (*A pause.*)

JIM. (*Gesturing at the cabinet.*) What do you need with mercuric chloride?

DOC. I used to use it for a disinfectant. I still do sometimes. I'm set in my ways. (*Jim turns and moves away, uncertain, then turns to Doc again.*)

JIM. Dora thinks the town is blessed, because the right people die. Lloyd Zachary, George Suggs . . .

DOC. The Reverend thinks that too. He's so complacent about God's love that it makes you wish for an earthquake.

JIM. But the right people *do* die.

DOC. So do the wrong people, like anywhere else.

JIM. There's nobody blind, nobody crippled.

DOC. It's a small town, with good Vermont stock. (*Goes to Jim and claps him fondly on the shoulder, laughing.*) Jimmy, Jimmy . . . I suppose I ought to be offended, being accused of killing off my patients, but I honestly can't bring myself to believe you mean what you're saying. How did you—get such an idea?

JIM. (*Not yet won over but wanting to be.*) I saw the R on some of the cards, and talking with Dora I realized they were people who—*should* have died. Except Darryl Maxim. And then Elias mentioned what R stood for.

DOC. In the garden.

JIM. In the garden . . .

DOC. (*Nods, smiles.*) Did Elias mention what T stands for?

JIM. Transplant?

DOC. That's right. And you'll find a lot of cards with T on them in the files, but none of my patients, to my knowledge, has ever been "transplanted." A lot of them, though, have been given tetanus shots. (*Pushes Jim on his way, smiling.*) Now take your things upstairs and get ready for dinner.

JIM. Why did you tell Darryl Maxim to rest when he was in perfect health? (*A pause.*)

DOC. In a minute I *am* going to get offended, Jimmy. Go on upstairs.

JIM. I'm not Jimmy any more, I'm another doctor. Questions have been raised in my mind, and unless you can satisfy me that

30

you're answering them truthfully, I'm—duty-bound to take them to—someone else.

DOC. "Duty-bound" . . .

JIM. Yes.

DOC. You really *are* twenty-seven years old, aren't you. (*Another clap on the shoulder.*) All right, Dr. Tennyson, just let me refresh my memory a bit. (*Going to the file.*) I can't remember everyone's history, as much as I'd like to. Maxim . . . (*Jim watches as Doc finds the card, takes it out, and comes* D. *studying it. After a moment:*) Let's see now . . . yes, I remember how it was. He came in and said he'd had a couple of dizzy spells. He hadn't told his wife because he didn't want to worry her. He hadn't told anyone else either. I gave him a quick check-over, which was negative, and he was going to call the next day and make an appointment for a full examination. He had to see when his next free time would be. In the meantime I told him to take things as easy as he could. (*Turns the card toward Jim.*) To rest. July twelfth, that was.

JIM. You didn't enter anything about the dizzy spells or the negative check-over.

DOC. It would have all been in the notes on the full examination. He didn't make the appointment, though, and two days later, on the fourteenth, he died.

JIM. Why didn't you give him a full examination when you had him here?

DOC. I couldn't; the waiting room was jam-packed. It would have taken over an hour. Are you satisfied?

JIM. No. I'm not. Dora said he came after office hours. Just around this time. (*The telephone rings. Doc backs to it, his eyes staying locked with Jim's. The telephone rings again. Doc picks up the receiver.*)

DOC. Yes? Yes. Is he in pain? No, not if he can walk on it. Just pack some ice around it and if it doesn't look any better in the morning, bring him in and I'll take an X-ray. Twenty minutes, half an hour. No, no, you didn't. Good-by. (*Hangs up. A pause.*) That's right. I'd forgotten. He came after hours and I didn't give him the full examination because I wanted to have Bea here to help with the tests. (*A pause.*)

JIM. Doc, please, level with me.

DOC. I *am* leveling with you.

JIM. (*Shakes his head.*) It doesn't *feel* that way.

DOC. Look, you of all people ought to believe me when I tell you something! And not—quiz me this way, cross-examine me as if I were—you had no business going into my files in the first place! That's a god-damn unprofessional thing to do!

JIM. I know, I know it is; I wish I hadn't.

DOC. Well . . . let's let—bygones be bygones, and forget all this—crap. And have the nice visit we were planning to have; what do you say, Jimmy?

JIM. How can we?

DOC. What do you mean? (*Jim looks at him wordlessly, then turns and goes L. to the foyer.*) Where are you going?

JIM. (*Gets his coat from the rack and turns, putting it on.*) Over to Elias's. I'm going to call—I don't know, the state police or the medical board or somebody; I don't know who.

DOC. You're going to make a fool of yourself.

JIM. I hope so.

DOC. You're going to get into trouble; I can promise you that! I'm not going to let anyone smear my name and get away with it, not even you! (*Jim picks up his suitcase and starts to go. Doc tries to maintain his show of anger but it cracks and goes and leaves him defenseless.*) Wait, wait. Wait a minute. All right. All right, come on back, Jim. Come on. Put it down. All right, I'll— level with you. Come on back. (*He backs R., gesturing appeasingly for Jim to follow. Jim, having turned, stands watching him.*) Come on. Put it down. I'll level with you. (*Sits on a hassock or low stool D. R.*) Come on. (*He rests his face in his hand for a moment, Jim slowly lowers his suitcase and stands feet-astride in the doorway, staring at Doc at a loss for understanding. Doc lowers his hand, looks at Jim, and looks away.*)

JIM. You've—killed people?

DOC. (*Nods.*) It's—what I told you before, about getting involved, caring what happens. When a Lloyd Zachary or a George Suggs is doing harm to the town—

JIM. There are *lawful ways of dealing with him.*

DOC. Twenty years we tried to deal lawfully with Lloyd Zachary!—tried to break up his bunch of tightwads and know-nothings and get ourselves a decent school! Twenty years! And every year a different legal maneuver up that frayed sleeve of his. So five hundred kids, and you're one of them, got less education

32

than they should have, and had to work harder for what little they got. I gave him every chance to square himself—pleaded publicly with him at meetings and privately here in this office; didn't make my mind up finally till 1961! And who misses him? Nobody. Not a damn soul.

JIM. What did you use?

DOC. I don't remember now. What difference does it make?

JIM. (*Moves a step closer to Doc.*) Did you give Susanna Booth a chance to square herself?

DOC. Oh Jimmy, that was a vegetable, not a child! She ate what was put in her mouth and went to sleep when she was put down. She didn't react or respond or even lift a hand of her own volition. And poor Barbara dressed her up once a week and tied a ribbon in her vegetable hair and sat her in a stroller and wheeled her into Simms' and the Bluebell, just daring anyone to see something wrong. It was a cloud over the town for two years. Perry thanked God when she died, and so did the grandparents. Every one did, and Barbara's glad now too.

JIM. (*A pause.*) Darryl Maxim caught on . . .

DOC. (*Nods gravely.*) That was—hard. He was a fine person and my real friend. I'd have sooner cut off my arm if I'd had the choice. The Reverend preached a stupid sermon about God's account books—a few weeks after George Suggs died—and Darryl came here and questioned me . . . (*He sits thinking, troubled, Jim moves another step closer to him.*)

JIM. How many, Doc? How many people have you—done it to?

DOC. (*Turns, looks at him.*) How many people's lives have I saved; first ask me that.

JIM. It's not relevant.

DOC. Not relevant? Why isn't saving a life relevant if taking one is? Helen Hart smashed into Earl Booth's truck last winter and was almost torn in two. Any doctor with a brain in his head would have let her go, she was that close to the edge. Not me though, not on your tintype! Eight straight hours I worked on her, piecing her back together again; and now she's alive and doing things, giving Elias his dinner this very minute!

JIM. Saving one life doesn't—

DOC. Old Man Beecher had a CA of the intestine eight or nine years ago! Bea says, "Doc, what are you killing yourself for?" Well he's a hundred and eight years old now, and tall and strong, and it makes you feel majestic just to look at him. That's what I was killing myself for.

JIM. Saving one life doesn't give you the right to take another. God Almighty, Doc, you know that!

DOC. No. One thing I know, one thing only! This town is the *happiest* town, and the *healthiest* town, in the entire state of Vermont! Maybe in the entire country! Maybe in the entire *world!* Now you just stop and think about that for a minute; the happiest, healthiest town in the entire world! It very well may be!

JIM. Not for Lloyd Zachary and—

DOC. (*On his feet.*) Lloyd Zachary gave up his right to be happy and healthy—

JIM. He *didn't!* He *didn't!*

DOC. —when he—he *did!*—when he deprived five hundred kids of a decent education!

JIM. That wasn't for you to decide!

DOC. Then who does decide if I don't? God and his account books? (*He waits; Jim is momentarily checked.*) Eh?

JIM. Nobody decides. You leave it to chance. Zachary was an ignorant bastard facing in the wrong direction but he was within his legal rights.

DOC. Tch! (*He turns scornfully away and moves u. Jim takes a following step.*)

JIM. How many? How many altogether?

DOC. (*At his desk, muttering.*) Go ahead, you keep quizzing me; this is really rich.

JIM. Zachary, Maxim, Susanna Booth, George Suggs, that Meserve woman—how many others? Dora mentioned a baby with a hump-back.

DOC. Don't let anybody ever tell you that there's no such thing as poetic justice in the world.

JIM. What do you mean?

DOC. That's what this is, you poking away at me like this: poetic justice, only I don't know who's giving it and who's getting it.

JIM. I don't understand what you're talking about.

DOC. Don't ask me; I might tell you.

JIM. Are you going to tell me how many others?

DOC. No. (*A pause.*)

JIM. Those poisons all leave traces. Everyone who died since you came here is going to be—disinterred and examined. (*Turns and starts toward the foyer.*)

DOC. IT WAS YOU WHO STARTED IT! (*Jim wheels.*) You —righteous—twenty-seven-year-old— It was you who started it!

JIM. (*A baffled whisper.*) *What are you talking about?*

DOC. Your arm! Your dripping mangled arm! And your mother, with the belt-buckle bruises on her stomach and her back! And your drunken hulk of a father! (*Jim stares mutely.*) What do you think he died of? *Your secret wishes?*

JIM. Cerebral hemorrhage . . .

DOC. *He died of my bottom shelf!* You—! And he was number one! The first! The beginning!

JIM. Oh Jesus no.

DOC. Oh Jesus yes! (*He paces around, bringing down the pitch of his anger. Jim stands motionless, eyes closed.*) Do you remember the other beatings he gave you? (*Jim nods.*) Every time she begged me not to tell; swore he was sorry, swore she'd keep him dry. She was afraid you'd be taken away from them, or he'd be *put* away and you'd have the shame to grow up with. But then the arm; I couldn't let that go by. I'd never cut down *any*one until then! Three, four, five times I'd seen situations where I could have, where I *should* have; where someone good was being hurt and mistreated. But I'd never had the nerve. Until then. Until I saw what he'd done to your arm.

JIM. I wanted him alive, so I could get bigger than he was.

DOC. You never would have made it; he'd have killed you before you were seven or eight. Or if you *had* made it, you'd be him all over again today: a millhand, drinking, giving a little boy what he gave you, and what his old man gave him. Beatings get handed down the same as land and money. So I killed him and you've grown up straight, and now you're a doctor, and you look at my records, and you quiz me, and you're going to go call the state police because it's wrong for me to kill. Do you see what I mean about poetic justice? (*Jim is staring at him, stunned. Doc goes to him and takes his arm earnestly in both hands.*) Never in anger, Jim. Never quickly. Never without months, sometimes *years*, of weighing, deciding. Always aware of the—awful responsibility, but accepting it; for the town, for Greenfield; to feed the good in it, to cut out the bad.

JIM. It's—a town, not a garden.

DOC. It's a perfect town. Why should a garden be perfect but not a town? People deserve more care than flowers do.

JIM. Than weeds do too.

DOC. No, no, Jim. Lives aren't all of them sacred. If you've got a gun and see a man stabbing a child, you shoot to stop him, don't you?

JIM. Yes.

DOC. If you've got cyanic acid and see a man beating a child and brutalizing him . . .

JIM. There are courts and judges.

DOC. But never enough justice! Look out there, no farther than Davistown and Hardwick; and look here, in Greenfield!

JIM. It's *wrong* . . .

DOC. Why? Because you've been *told* it's wrong since you were two years old? It's *right!* The proof is in the town; the happiness, the *love;* the way they all flock into church on Sundays and sing their thanks up to heaven. And let me tell you this, Jimmy: every doctor does it, more or less. When it's a Helen Hart who's almost dead, you break your back to save her; when it's a Lloyd Zachary, you don't.

JIM. No—

DOC. Just wait. Wait. Wait till you're on your own, just you and the patient, with no resident peeping over your shoulder.

JIM. You do your best for everyone.

DOC. I'd have said so too, at twenty-seven. Just wait. You'll make your choices. We all make choices. (*Moving away from Jim,* u. *toward his desk or the* Flower and Garden *cover.*) I'm not so unique. A little more willing to shoulder responsibility than most men, but not so unique, no . . .

JIM. (*Watches him.*) How many, Doc?

DOC. (*Turning.*) How many what?

JIM. People.

DOC. Oh. Thirty.

JIM. (*A pause.*) Thirteen?

DOC. No, thirty. In twenty-one years. Hurt people. People who'd been hurt so badly and for so long that all they could finally do was hurt other people. Your father and Bruce Hart and Hannah Meserve. Ned Ingles, P. T. Fletcher . . . and some who were in terrible pain and for whom there was no hope, and they were draining the life and the happiness of the people around them.

36

Reba Sanford and Sax Rousseau. Fred Allbright. No, it was Leonard. Leonard Allbright.

JIM. Who else?

DOC. Children. Oh, those are the ones I hate to think about. Susanna Booth, and the McClure baby—that was the humpbacked one—and a monstrous baby that Ruth Scudder had when Bob was in Korea, and Reuben Wilcox.

JIM. Because of his legs?

DOC. That's right.

JIM. (*A pause.*) Who else, Doc?

DOC. The troublemakers. Mack Bullit. Diana Rausch.

JIM. George Suggs.

DOC. No! He really had empyema! (*Laughs, points upward.*) God finally took a look at the account books! Isn't that a laugh? And that was the one that made Darryl suspicious! (*The laugh ends and he grows sober again.*) And before Darryl there was Ted Ruth senior.

JIM. He got suspicious too?

DOC. (*Nods.*) I'd sooner have cut off my right arm if I'd had any choice about it. Ted was my good friend, you know. He's the one who made my greenhouse in there.

JIM. (*Pause.*) Who else?

DOC. Let's see now . . .

JIM. My mother? So I'd have the insurance money?

DOC. *What are you talking about?* No! Are you crazy?

JIM. I don't know! I don't know, Doc! I don't know *who* died naturally!

DOC. You *saw* how I sweated over her, didn't you? Weren't you beside me, helping me? I was going to give you the money for school, you know that. I *cherished* your mother! Orrin Sanderson! He was taking eight- and nine-year-old girls into that shed behind his shop. *That's* what I pull out, not someone like your mother! I *cherished* her! Joe Schmidt! And the handyman at Grievers', I've got his name there, the Polish one. (*Sits* R. *tiredly.*) And that couple who came here from Canada. Jefferson. Herb and Dorothy. They weren't husband and wife, they were brother and sister. She confessed it to me when she got pregnant. That isn't all thirty, is it?

JIM. No.

DOC. Did I mention Mack Bullit?

JIM. Yes.

DOC. Never in anger, Jimmy. And never quickly. This is the best town in the whole state, and you know it. And that's not just Chamber of Commerce talk either. (*He sits silently brooding. Jim closes his eyes for a moment, then draws a breath, blows it out, and opens his eyes. He looks at Doc.*)

JIM. Doc . . . (*Doc looks at him.*) There's so much that I owe you—

DOC. That's the truth, Jim.

JIM. I don't mean—my father. I mean—the things you taught me, the—the image you gave me of what I might some day be . . . look, this has to stop. *You* think it's right but it's wrong. The law says it's wrong and *I* say it's wrong, and I'm not going to debate it with you, I'm just going to tell you that it has to stop. Completely. The *garden* is your garden, not the town. The garden. And it ends at the picket fences. Now nothing on earth is going to bring any one of those thirty people back to life again, so because of what I owe you, and because I love you, and because the town needs you *when you're being the doctor and not the judge and the jury*—because of those reasons I'm going to keep my mouth shut, but *only on one condition*. Do you understand? I'm going to become an accessory, after all your thirty facts, but only on one condition, no *two* conditions. (*Goes closer to him, pointing.*) One: you've got to give me your solemn vow right here and now that you're never going to poison anyone ever again, never going to *kill* anyone ever again in any way or by any means. And two: we've got to work out some kind of way for me to be sure that you're—fulfilling your vow. Not because I don't trust you, but because—well we've *got* to, that's all. Otherwise I can't keep quiet. All right?

DOC. What happens to the town?

JIM. What do you mean?

DOC. What happens to the town? What keeps it from going to seed?

JIM. Doc, *gardens* go to seed. Towns—muddle along. All right, somebody is going to be in pain. A kid is going to have a father who breaks his arm and kicks him. Somebody is going to— maybe fool around with little girls. Doc, those are things that are *not* as bad as killing. The town can take care of them legally. And the things the town *can't* take care of—it will simply have to live with and get used to. Boy oh boy, if you lived in Chicago! (*Pantomiming it broadly.*) Twenty-eight hours a day you'd be handing out the strychnine and the arsenic! Okay?

DOC. I don't have any choice, do I?

JIM. No, I guess you don't.

DOC. (*Rising.*) All right, you've got my word.

JIM. I want to hear it.

DOC. I said you've got it.

JIM. I want to hear it, Doc!

DOC. (*A pause.*) I swear I won't poison anyone—

JIM. Won't kill anyone!

DOC. —won't kill anyone ever again. In any way or by any means.

JIM. (*A pause.*) All right. (*He realizes that he has his coat on and takes it off. Doc watches him.*)

DOC. And what are you going to do, go on my rounds with me?

JIM. That's a good question; what am I going to do. (*Thinks, dropping his coat over a chair.*) Okay, I'll tell you what I'm going to do. I'm going to have the *Courier* sent to me every week and I'm going to read it very carefully, especially the obituaries. And I'm going to keep in touch, with the Reverend and Ray Higley. I'm going to know what's going on. And I'm going to visit, every couple of months or so. If the right people keep on dying, or if I even *suspect* that the right people are dying, then I'm going to tell. There'll still be plenty of proof up at the cemetery; at least in the last few arrivals, there will.

DOC. The thing for me to do now, I guess, is remove some of the *wrong* people.

JIM. You remove nobody ever again. Don't you forget it.

DOC. I was making a joke, that's all.

JIM. (*Looks at him for a moment.*) Christ Almighty, Doc. If people ever found out . . . ! (*Shakes his head.*)

DOC. Make no mistake; plenty of them would thank me.

JIM. (*Nods.*) Some would, I suppose.

DOC. A *lot* would. Plenty! The whole damn town! (*A pause.*)

JIM. I want the key, Doc.

DOC. The key?

JIM. To the cabinet.

DOC. You've got my vow.

JIM. I want the key too. Tonight or tomorrow we'll go through

39

that stuff down there and get rid of what you don't really need. And we'll measure out what you *do* really need and you're going to have to keep a record for me of what happens to every last grain and particle. (*Puts his hand out for the key.*) I'm sorry, Doc. It's the only way. (*A pause, and then Doc takes a key-chain from his pocket and ruefully begins detaching one of the keys.*)

DOC. My young helper Jimmy is taking my key from me . . .

JIM. Life's little ironies. (*Doc detaches the key and puts it on Jim's palm. Jim holds and examines it, looks at the cabinet.*)

DOC. It's the right one. (*Jim looks at Doc and pockets the key.*)

JIM. I'll give it back when we've—cleaned things out. (*Doc turns and moves away, his hands in his pockets. He looks older, resentful.*) What it all comes down to simply is—the good old end doesn't justify the good old means. You've got a whole town ecstatically happy, in neat rows with no bugs and no crabgrass; but thirty people are lying in the cemetery and they didn't get a chance to say one word in their own behalf. Who knows? Maybe I was one of the many small boys who *deserve* to be kicked and beaten. (*Doc doesn't smile, he rocks on his heels, unforgiving.*) Well, debate ended. You garden in the garden. (*Jim picks up his coat and goes L. Doc turns.*)

DOC. Are you going?

JIM. No. Do you want me to?

DOC. No.

JIM. I could stay with Ray and Jean.

DOC. (*Letting go his resentment.*) No, no; don't be silly. (*Jim goes to the coat rack and hangs up his coat. He turns toward Doc again in the foyer doorway.*)

JIM. I don't feel any differently toward you, Doc; damned if I know why, but I don't. Maybe I will in a week or so, I don't know. I hope not. And I hope you don't feel any differently toward me.

DOC. Of course I don't, Jimmy. (*Smiles.*) I'm just a little sorry I didn't chase you home all those times your mother said I should.

JIM. (*Smiling back.*) You and Dr. Frankenstein, turned upon by your own creations.

DOC. I didn't create you, Jimmy; you know that. If I helped a little, then I'm still glad and still proud.

JIM. Thank you, Doc. (*Picks up his suitcase.*) I'll go unpack.

40

(*He goes quickly up the stairs and out of sight. Doc's smile fades away, he comes* D. *and stands troubled and brooding, his fists in his pockets. He sniffs, thinks, rocks on his heels, frowns. After a moment the telephone rings. Doc doesn't seem to hear. He thinks more, sniffs again, worries. The telephone rings again. Doc goes back to the desk and without breaking out of his mood takes up the receiver.*)

DOC. Yes? Oh. Yes, he is. He—he just went upstairs, Ray. He was going to call you and Jean and then we got talking and— Ray. Hold on, will you? Just hold on a minute. (*He lays the receiver on the desk, looks up at the stairs, and goes quietly across the office to the waiting room. He closes the connecting door partway, looks out, and then takes up the receiver of the reception-desk telephone. He is genuinely upset and perturbed.*) Ray? I'm in the waiting room now. I don't want Jim to hear me. I—I don't know what to say, Ray. I don't know what to tell you. He's so dear to me. He's like a *son* to me, you know that. And I'm—I'm afraid there's something wrong with him! I know I shouldn't say anything, but he looks so fine, so apparently healthy, and while we were talking he got this—what looked like some kind of cerebrovascular disturbance. His speech got all jumbled and meaningless and he wasn't even aware of it. And his father died of a cerebral hemorrhage—you remember, Ray?—and before he did, he had the same kind of disturbances. When I think that Jimmy may end up the same way his father did, I'd sooner cut off my arm. I swear that's the truth, Ray; I'd sooner cut off my arm! Listen, Ray; I'm being foolish and a—a foolish man. I'm sure he's all right. Forget what I said, will you? (*Another look out through the doorway.*) He's just been pushing so hard, that's what it is, with the interning—you can't imagine what a grind that is—and then the examinations right after, and now he's got some kind of appeal pending with his draft board. I'm *sure* he is. Don't upset Jean, now. Don't say anything to *her*. He'll probably call you later on and—yes, yes. You too, Ray, you too. Good-by. (*He hangs up and stands thinking unhappily for a moment, then looks into the office again and opens the door and goes on. Going to the desk, he quietly hangs up the telephone there, looks up toward the top of the stairs, listens. He thinks again, and reaches a reluctant decision. Going* D. R., *he stands on tiptoes and, from atop a high book or door frame, takes an unseeable something with*

41

which he goes D. L. *He crouches and—the something is a key—unlocks the drug cabinet. He takes a small bottle from the bottom shelf, inspects it thoughtfully, then takes out a second bottle, weighs them, and puts back the first. He closes the door, reopens it, rearranges the bottles so that no gap is visible among them, then closes the door again and locks it. Rising, he goes D. R. again and returns the key to its hiding place. Jim calls from upstairs.*)

JIM. Doc? (*Doc goes near his desk and stands facing the stairs, holding the small bottle behind his back in one hand.*)

DOC. Yes? What is it? (*Jim comes down the stairs far enough to see and be seen.*)

JIM. Do I have time to take a shower and put on a clean shirt?

DOC. Sure. Of course. Go ahead, Jim.

JIM. I'll be as quick as I can. (*He goes up and out of sight again.*)

DOC. Don't rush. Whenever you're ready—that's when we'll eat. (*He exits quickly, determinedly, into the kitchen as the curtain falls.*)

END OF ACT TWO

ACT III

AT RISE: *Half an hour later. Jim is standing by the desk laughing into the telephone. He is combed and clean looking in a fresh sport shirt, and has a napkin in his hand. Doc is sitting at the desk quietly eating a plate of stew. A second plate, half eaten, is on the hassock or low stool D. R., which is serving as table to a nearby chair. Outside the house there is total darkness.*

JIM. (*Laughing.*) You didn't! To all three cars? (*Laughs more.*) You're a nut, you're an absolute nut! (*And a little more.*) How does Fran feel about it? Well, good for her. She's a nut too. No, not tonight; there are—things Doc and I want to talk about. Look, why don't you come by in the morning, around nine or so, and you can run me out to South Green. I want to see Charley and Chris and— Perfect. I'll see you then. So long, nutto. (*Hangs up and laughs.*) Did you hear how he let Rudy know he was quitting?

DOC. (*Nodding, smiling.*) Yes, I did. We all did.

JIM. He should have done it long ago.

DOC. He never should have started working there at all. He's capable of much more than fixing cars.

JIM. You've got to hand it to him; it takes nerve to change now, with a wife and a child and another on the way. (*A pause, as he thinks about it.*)

DOC. You haven't finished your stew.

JIM. Oh. Yeh. (*Doc watches as Jim goes D. R. and suddenly turns.*) Listen, would you like me to stay around and give you a hand tomorrow morning?

DOC. No.

JIM. 'Cause I can go to South Green in the afternoon just as well.

DOC. No, no, go in the morning, the way you planned.

JIM. (*Sitting.*) Bob's free all day, so just say the word and—

DOC. No, really, there's no need for you to—stay around. (*Jim takes a fork from the plate.*) Things are quiet now anyway. (*Jim*

43

forks up a piece of stew and puts it into his mouth. Doc watches, then follows suit. Both chew, and it might be noted at this moment that their plates are of different colors. Jim swallows.)

JIM. What was I telling you? Oh, my nemesis, Dr. Kalebjian.

DOC. And the woman whose pressure dropped.

JIM. Mm. Well it was way down—ninety over forty or something —and she was just barely breathing. With an IV running, glucose and water. *(He takes another bite, Doc watches.)* According to the chart Kalebjian had given me, she had a couple of pints of blood on stand-by and she was slated for a bone marrow biopsy in the morning. Now what am I supposed to do?

DOC. If you give her the blood, the biopsy has to be postponed.

JIM. Exactly. *(Another bite.)* So I'm standing there trying to make up my mind when suddenly I notice that there's no IV ordered on the chart. There it is stuck in her arm but it's not on the chart. And according to the work-up she's forty-four years old, and this woman I'm looking at is— *(The telephone rings. Doc picks up the receiver.)*

DOC. Yes? Hello. How are you? I'm sorry to hear that, Livvy. Is it as severe as last time? *(Jim goes on eating.)* No, that doesn't necessarily follow. Do you still have the drops? You take three of them in a glass of water and get into bed. Janet's there, isn't she? You do as I say and don't worry. I'll look in some time tomorrow afternoon. Only if you can't sleep, but you'll sleep fine, you'll see. Of course I won't. Good-by. *(Hangs up, takes his pen and jots a note.)* Livvy Sawyer.

JIM. How old is she now?

DOC. *(Swinging around toward Jim.)* One hundred and two years.

JIM. That's great.

DOC. *(Meaningfully.)* She had uremia three years ago, and hepatitis and cirrhosis before that. *(A pause.)*

JIM. Doc, I know there are dozens of people who would be dead now if it weren't for you. That's true of every doctor. I've even saved one life that everyone had pretty much given up on. *(Doc eats.)* Does every doctor have the right to kill?

DOC. This is a *special situation here*, where I know the whole town inside and out!

JIM. Does every Vermont doctor who's the only doctor in his *town* have the—

44

DOC. *There's no point in talking about it now.*

JIM. There is. There is, though. I don't want you feeling resentful and angry at me.

DOC. There's no point in talking about it.

JIM. There *is*, Doc. (*He sniffs at a fork of stew and eats it, fleetingly it doesn't taste as it should, but then it does. Doc watches with sharpened interest for a moment.*)

DOC. I'm not angry at you, Jim.

JIM. You just sounded angry.

DOC. No, I can see how someone your age would automatically take the conventional view . . .

JIM. For Pete's sake, Doc, it has nothing to do with my age and nothing to do with convention! It's a matter of logic and— (*Someone has tried the door* L.*, found it locked, and now the doorbell rings—one of the old-fashioned turnscrew kind. Doc looks around and sits motionless.*) Did you lock the door already?

DOC. Yes. (*A pause.*)

JIM. Shall I—?

DOC. (*Rising quickly.*) I'll get it, you stay. (*He goes into the foyer and unlocks and unbolts the front door. Elias is outside.*)

ELIAS. You locked up early.

DOC. Jim and I are talking.

ELIAS. I've got something for him. For you too.

DOC. Thanks. I'll—

ELIAS. Let me bring it in. It's more for him than for you. (*Doc stands aside and Elias comes in, carrying a napkin-covered pie plate.*)

JIM. Hi.

ELIAS. It looks like I timed this just right. (*Doc closes the front door and comes to the foyer doorway. Elias stands before Jim.*) Guess what it is.

JIM. A pie.

ELIAS. What kind?

JIM. (*Thinks.*) Pumpkin?

ELIAS. No . . . Helen's own peach! (*Uncovering it.*) From out of the freezer and part of it eaten, and we both apologize to you.

JIM. Apologize? That's great! Boy, I haven't seen anything so beautiful in years!

ELIAS. (*Including Doc in his explanation.*) She took it out yesterday and we had some last night, and all through supper just now she was fretting and upset that she hadn't thought to take out two. "I'll bring them what's left of this one," I says, but she says no, you can't bring someone half a pie. "Why not?" I says. "It's the same as with bread. Half a pie is better than none the same as half a loaf is!"

JIM. You were absolutely right! Thanks a million. And thank Helen too.

ELIAS. I'll put it over here; you go on eating. Doc, go on eating; don't let me interrupt you. (*He puts the pie in an out-of-the-way place. Doc moves reluctantly toward the desk.*) While I'm here I've got a question I want to ask you, Jimmy.

JIM. (*Eating.*) What's that?

ELIAS. A little thing that's been annoying me. I'm getting to be like you, Doc, wanting to be sure everything is settled and orderly the way it's supposed to be.

JIM. What is it?

ELIAS. You said before that you saw one of the markers—one of the stickers I told you about—you said you saw one with an R on it and that was how you knew R was one of the letters in Doc's and my code that we use.

JIM. (*A pause.*) That's right.

ELIAS. Well where is it? Because I couldn't find it when I went out of here. It was still light enough to see and I looked all over the front. (*To Doc.*) I thought I was finally caught up with things, except for the yew tree. Did Jim tell you about that?

DOC. Yes.

ELIAS. I'll come by around three or four.

DOC. That'll be fine.

ELIAS. Where was it, Jim? The sticker you saw.

JIM. On one of the bushes.

DOC. I took it off. I went out on a call after Jim came in and I stopped and took it off. It was on one of the dwarf lilacs but I changed my mind.

ELIAS. You think there's too many?

DOC. No. I did, but I changed my mind.

ELIAS. Well that explains it. (*To Jim.*) I was going to come back in right then and ask you, only Helen started waving to me from the porch. It bothered me though, not finding it, and that as much as the pie is why I came over.

DOC. (*Smiling.*) And now you've taken care of both reasons.

ELIAS. That's right, so I'll get out of your way and let you go on with your supper.

DOC. No, no . . . (*Jim breathes deeply and slaps his chest. Elias and Doc look at him.*)

JIM. I'm short of breath.

ELIAS. You mustn't eat too fast.

DOC. Thank Helen for the pie, will you, Elias?

ELIAS. Sure thing.

JIM. Tell her that—(*Another deep breath.*)—half of one of her peach pies is better than all of anyone else's.

ELIAS. (*Backing R.*) Right. Come visit with us when you're done, why don't you? Have you seen any color TV yet, Jim?

JIM. A little.

DOC. (*Following along with Elias.*) We'll try, but don't count on us.

ELIAS. If not, I'll see you tomorrow.

JIM. Good night. Thanks again!

DOC. (*Seeing Elias out the door.*) Good night, Elias. Thank you.

ELIAS. (*Out of sight.*) Don't even mention it, Doc. (*Doc closes the door and locks it and bolts it. Jim considers another forkful of stew, decides against it, and puts the fork down on his plate. He sits without moving, puzzled by his shortness of breath. Doc comes to the foyer doorway and looks at him.*)

DOC. You didn't finish telling me about Dr.—I don't remember his name.

JIM. (*A pause.*) Kalebjian . . . Wolf N. Kalebjian . . .

DOC. That's quite a monicker.

JIM. (*Another pause. Not looking at Doc.*) The woman was— according to the chart she was supposed to be forty-four. But the woman on the bed looked—late fifties, almost sixty. (*Doc moves D. R., ostensibly listening to Jim's slow, numbed narration. He draws a window shade, closes curtains.*) And the chart said— five feet six, but the woman was shorter than that—about five-two. (*A pause. Jim looks at Doc, who stands casually by the covered window. Jim squints uncomfortably at him.*) Would you turn the lamp off, please? My eyes hurt.

DOC. Sure, Jim. (*Doc turns the lamp off.*)

JIM. Thank you.

DOC. You're welcome.

47

JIM. (*A pause.*) All of a sudden—it dawned on me—that he had given me—the wrong chart.

DOC. (*Crossing quietly* u. *of Jim.*) Do you think he did it on purpose?

JIM. Of course he did. He never made a mistake in his whole life, the—

DOC. (*Drawing the shade and curtains of a window* L. *more openly than before.*) He probably did it to see if you would notice.

JIM. (*Nods.*) That's what he said when I—went back to him on it. He was "testing" me. (*Doc goes into the waiting room. He closes curtains and checks the lock and bolt of the rear door.*) But that was no time for testing. I think he wanted me to give that woman the other woman's two pints of blood. It wouldn't have hurt her any, her pressure so low—they were the same type— but it would have got me into—(*Doc comes back into the office and stands listening to Jim.*)—six kinds of trouble with—Harris and Benjamin.

DOC. (*A pause.*) Shall I turn this lamp off too?

JIM. (*Turns, grimaces.*) Please. (*Doc turns a second lamp off. Jim rubs his closed eyes.*) I don't know what it is, that's made my eyes so sensitive . . . (*Doc picks up Jim's plate with the fork on it, and puts a hand on Jim's shoulder.*)

DOC. I'm going to take the plates into the kitchen now and get the coffee. You sit right here and wait for me—(*A glimmer of pained sympathy.*)—all right, Jimmy?

JIM. Sure, Doc.

DOC. I'll just be a minute or two. (*Goes to the desk, picks up his own plate and fork, and continues* u. L.) You stay right there. (*He goes out into the kitchen. Jim sits motionless for a moment.*)

JIM. She was Dr. Benjamin's patient . . . (*A pause, and then he blinks, frowns, and feels his heart. He takes his pulse, and after a few seconds of soundless counting realizes that it's far slower than it ought to be. He looks about, rises, licks his lips. He looks toward the kitchen, could it be? He goes to the drug cabinet, tries it, finds it locked, stands uncertainly, then searches in his pockets and finds the key. He unlocks the cabinet, locks and unlocks the opened door, stands straight and calls out in frightened confusion.*) Doc? (*No answer. He gasps for breath, then turns, drops to his knees by the cabinet and pulls bottle after bottle from the bottom shelf, trying to find one missing or disturbed. He gives up, and gasping—nearly suffocating—rises and turns to the sliding doors of the examining room. He tries to pull one open, it sticks, he pulls harder, strains, it flies open and Doc stands before him. Jim falls back, startled. Doc comes out, tense, keyed up.)*

DOC. Sit down, Jimmy. Sit down over there. That's right. *(Jim sits u. c., gasping. Doc glances at the opened cabinet.)* Did you figure out what I gave you? Sodium cyanide. *(Takes the bottle from his pocket, shows it.)* See? It's slower than potassium cyanide but faster than anything else except cyanic acid. *(Jim groans, gasps. Doc puts the poison back in the cabinet.)* You'll have some convulsions in a minute or two and then you'll go into a gradual paralysis and then you'll die. The antidote is inside there—don't move! It's all ready in a pan; a shot of sodium nitrite, and another of sodium thiosulfate, and amyl nitrite for inhalation.

JIM. Doc! Please, Doc! I beg you!

DOC. You forced me into this. I don't enjoy scaring you this way, maybe killing you. You're almost my son. But what am I supposed to do? Let you come in here and ruin the whole town? After all the love and the labor I've put into it? Over thirty years I've been working here! *(Jim gives an agonized gasp and undergoes a violent racking convulsion. Doc leans forward and watches compassionately. When the final spasm ends, Jim is sprawled limp and sweating in the chair.)* That's the worst, Jim. The first one's the strongest and then they get weaker.

JIM. I'll go away. I won't come back. I won't say a word to anyone. I swear to God!

DOC. Security! I've got to have some kind of security! I can't just take your word, don't you see that? *(Moves his chair a bit closer to Jim.)* What I'm hoping, praying, is that you've got something *you* don't want told, just the way I do!

JIM. Something I—

DOC. Something secret! Something people might not understand about, and then I can forgive you and trust you and give you the antidote. Tell me something, Jim. I don't take pleasure in killing. *(Jim cries out and undergoes a second convulsion, shorter and less violent than the first. Doc watches, waits, moves a bit closer.)* Tell me something. Did you try drugs at the hospital?

49

JIM. No.

DOC. Did you steal anything? Sell anything?

JIM. I—I did—

DOC. Did what?

JIM. Did an abortion, on Liz.

DOC. Your girl?

JIM. Yes.

DOC. When?

JIM. Last June.

DOC. Where?

JIM. In the hospital. Sneaked her in. Nurses helped me.

DOC. You performed the abortion in the hospital?

JIM. Yes.

DOC. It was your baby?

JIM. Yes.

DOC. (*A pause.*) Is this the truth, Jim?

JIM. Have proof. Letters where she mentions it. She went home after. Wrote to me. Have them here. (*A third convulsion, shorter and less racking than the second. After it, Jim sprawls motionless, as a general paralysis begins setting in. His speech becomes slower and slurred, seemingly disinterested, his eyes close and his breathing becomes quick and shallow.*)

DOC. (*Warily.*) You have the letters here?

JIM. My suitcase . . . lent my room to a friend . . . was afraid he might find them . . . (*Doc backs toward the foyer.*)

DOC. Where in your suitcase?

JIM. Side pocket . . . blue envelopes . . . three blue envelopes . . . (*Doc backs farther, onto the first step of the stairs. He watches Jim, who lies motionless, eyes closed, gasping weakly. After a moment Doc comes down off the step. He puts the bottle on the desk and goes into the examining room. He comes out with a white enamel pan and, not hurrying, goes to Jim's side and puts the pan somewhere handy. He takes a capsule from it and breaks it at Jim's nostrils. He lifts Jim's head. Jim winces, moans.*)

DOC. Come on, breathe it in . . . (*He waits a moment and then lowers Jim's head and throws the capsule into the pan. He undoes Jim's left cuff, pushes up the sleeve, and ties a length of rubber tubing around the arm. He takes a syringe from the pan, tries it, and injects it below the tubing. When the syringe is empty he draws it out, puts it in the pan, unties the tubing, and rubs and flexes Jim's arms. Jim watches him.)* Don't worry, you'll be all right. It would take more than a little sodium cyanide to knock off a bozo like you . . . *(Undoes the other cuff, pushes up the sleeve and, taking a second syringe from the pan, goes around to Jim's other side.)* That was the nitrite, this is the thiosulfate. *(Ties on the tubing.)* In case you care . . . *(Tests the syringe and injects it, then draws it out, unties the tubing, rubs the arm.)* Abortion right in the hospital; you're a pretty nervy young fellow. *(Reaching over Jim, he puts the second syringe and the tubing into the pan and then flexes both Jim's arms simultaneously.)* Not as smart as you should have been, though. You know how many keys I've got to that cabinet? Four. The one I carry, one on top of the books there, one up in my bedroom—*(Tries Jim's pulse.)*—and one in a little magnet-thing stuck up inside the fender of the car, along with an extra set of car keys. It's getting to you, isn't it?

JIM. Mm.

DOC. *(Going back around him.)* In half an hour you'll be yourself again. Do you know much about poisons and antidotes?

JIM. Mm-mmn. *(Doc breaks another capsule at Jim's nostrils; Jim raises his head a bit and breathes deeply of it.)* Ooof!

DOC. *(Helping him sit erect, holding the capsule.)* Oh, I'm glad you told me what you did so I could spare you, Jimmy! Seeing you die would have been terrible. I'd always rather be merciful than cruel, but most times there's just no room for choice. We're better friends now than we were before, aren't we? Because we know about each other, we don't have any secrets between us! That's rare, that's a rare condition, Jimmy. Listen, I want to tell you one more thing. I worry. I do. Because I'm human, you know, I'm not God. I have my emotions. And there's an element of *pleasure* that enters into killing someone—even when it's done for valid reasons—there's an element of pleasure in making the decision and carrying it out and being triumphant and still alive— and sometimes I worry, in the case of Herb and Dorothy Jefferson, for instance, I worry that the element of pleasure might be playing a part in my decisions. But incest is wrong biologically, not only morally, isn't it? *(Jim nods.)* Or Laura Scoville. Now a teen-age girl, especially a pretty one, she's *always* going to bring emotion into the picture and complicate things, isn't she?

51

JIM. (*A pause.*) What did she do?

DOC. Laura?

JIM. Yes.

DOC. (*A pause. He puts aside the capsule.*) Well, that's something I'd rather not go into, Jim. It's really not important. What *is* important is that pleasure didn't enter into my decision, because if it had, if pleasure were a factor of any importance at all, then I would have killed *you*, right?

JIM. Right.

DOC. I would have sat there and watched you gasping and sweating and I wouldn't have given you any chance at all to save yourself. But I did, I had mercy on you, and now you're looking much better, young Dr. Tennyson! How do you feel?

JIM. (*Watching Doc.*) Dead.

DOC. You were an interesting shade of blue there for a few minutes. Can you move your legs? (*Still watching Doc, Jim weakly lifts one foot and then the other.*) That's fine. Do you know what we have to do now?

JIM. What?

DOC. Wash out your stomach. I'm sorry, but we do. I'll go get things ready. Don't try to walk yet. Here, sniff a little more. (*Taking the pan, he gives Jim one of the capsules and goes R.; gestures toward the cabinet and turns.*) I had the potassium cyanide in my hand, you know that? And I thought, no, no, that's too quick. Even then I meant to be fair with you and give you a chance . . . (*He turns again and goes into the examining room and out of sight. Jim sits listening, the capsule to his nose.*) If I didn't show mercy to *you*, I'd be a pretty unspeakable creature, wouldn't I? Even *with* the whole town at stake. (*He falls silent. There are sounds of a drawer being opened and closed, of water running. Quietly Jim rises from his chair. He leans unsteadily against it, takes a final sniff at the capsule and puts it down. Doc calls from the examining room.*) How are you doing?

JIM. A little better! (*Begins making his way to the waiting room, holding on to one piece of furniture and then another.*)

DOC. I want you to stay the weekend the way you planned, otherwise everyone's going to wonder. You can leave on Monday morning. (*Jim makes his way through the waiting room to the door.*) I'll be ready in a minute. Keep sniffing the amyl. (*Jim tries the door, finds it locked. He unlocks it and tries it again*

52

but it still won't open.) I had to do this to a three-year-old boy yesterday. Jill Stormer's little fellow. Swallowed some furniture polish. (*Jim is reaching up to open a bolt high on the door when Doc comes out of the examining room. Jim freezes in the near-darkness.*) It took Jill and Bea and Dora to hold the poor kid down while I— (*He sees the empty chair, glances R. and moves to look up the stairwell. Then he turns and looks L. and grows chill and hostile.*) What are you doing there?

JIM. Going. Isn't that what you want?

DOC. I want you to stay the weekend. Otherwise everyone's going to wonder.

JIM. (*A pause.*) I'm going.

DOC. To—tell . . .

JIM. Doc . . . you need help.

DOC. (*Pointing upstairs.*) I'll show those letters!

JIM. There are no letters. No abortion. (*He turns and unbolts the door. Erupting into fury, Doc races across the office, through the waiting room, and catches Jim with both hands by the back of his shirt. He swings him around and hurls him forward—into the office, where he falls on hands and knees. Doc is right after him, kicking at him.*)

DOC. *Liar! You liar!* THOU SHALT NOT LIE! (*He locks his fists and raises them to club Jim's head, but Jim catches him around the waist and tries to bear him downward. They grapple. After a few moments Doc succeeds in working free and landing a blow that sends Jim sprawling on his back. Doc throws himself on him, grabs a cushion from the davenport, and clamps it over Jim's face, holding it with all his strength against the weak flailing of Jim's arms. At first it seems as if Jim will be suffocated, but after several futile tries he manages to get his arms between Doc's and throws him off. Doc climbs to his feet and looks about for a weapon, breathing curses. Jim rolls over and drags himself to the desk. Doc gets a metal ashstand from the waiting room, as Jim, by the desk, reaches up. Doc swings, Jim ducks away, and the ashstand strikes the desktop. Jim grabs the shank of the stand and pulls himself up to his feet. The two men struggle for the ashstand, and finally Jim wrests it from Doc and falls back a few steps, holding it before him in readiness. Doc snatches up a letter opener from the desk but drops it, suddenly open-mouthed. He puts both hands to his chest and turns wide-*

eyed to Jim.) Heart! (*Jim stands motionless, caught up short.*)
Real. Real. (*Collapses into the desk chair, pale, sweating.*) Tablets. Cabinet. Nitroglycerin. (*Jim puts down the ashstand.*) **Top**
shelf. Quick. Bad one. (*Activated, Jim steps to the cabinet and
finds the right bottle on the top shelf. Doc winces with pain.*)
Quick. Two of them.

JIM. (*Trying to uncap the bottle.*) I can't get it—(*Stops. Looks
at Doc. A pause.*)—open . . . (*Their eyes lock, and then Jim
drops back a step.*)

DOC. Jim. Please. Be merciful. I was merciful to you, wasn't I?
Now you be merciful to me. (*He gasps at the worsening pain.
There are tears in his eyes. Jim takes another step away from
him.*)

JIM. Oh God, Doc, I think that's what I'm doing!

DOC. (*Almost laughs.*) Jimmy, little Jimmy . . . you see? You
see—how it—begins? (*He slips forward to his knees, then tumbles
sideward and lies still. Jim looks at him, looks at the bottle in his
hand. He is stunned, in a turmoil. He puts the bottle back on the
shelf, goes hesitantly to Doc and stands looking down at him.
He crouches, feels Doc's chest, tries his pulse. Rising, he thinks
and then goes unsteadily into the foyer. He unlocks and unbolts
the front door. Opening it, he cups his hands and shouts at the
top of his lungs.*)

JIM. E-LI-AS! (*Listens for a moment and then goes back into the
office and to the desk, picks up the phone and jiggles the crossbar.*) Zenia? Ring Elias Hart, will you please? Yes, it is. Please,
get Elias. It's urgent. (*Listens, tries to compose himself.*) Elias?
Yes, I did. Listen, something's happened here. Doc has—had a
heart attack. Yes. Yes, very. He's dead. We were—(*Stops, looks
about, thinks.*)—we were—*talking* about how it was when *he*
was an intern, and he started laughing at this story he told me,
he started laughing very, very hard . . . all right, please do.
(*He bangs up. A pause, and then he sets hastily to work. He
closes and locks the cabinet, weighs the key, and goes to Doc
and crouches by him. He tucks the key into Doc's pocket and
minimizes the disarray of Doc's hair and clothes. Rising, he picks
up the ashstand and brings it back to its place in the waiting
room. He puts the cushion back on the davenport and sets the
furniture as it was before the fight. Hearing Elias approaching, he
hurriedly puts right the last sign of the fight, takes a position*

54

near Doc's body, and tucks in his shirt and smooths down his hair. Elias comes to the part-way-open front door and enters. He comes into the office, looks at Doc and wordlessly, painfully, at Jim.) He had an attack before. Bea knows about it.

ELIAS. I do too. She told me. (*Looks down at Doc again.*) God help us now. (*And up at Jim.*) Was it Zenia on the board when you called me?

JIM. Yes.

ELIAS. We'd better put something over him. The whole town's going to be here in a minute. (*Jim weaves unsteadily.*) Are you all right, Jim?

JIM. No, not completely.

ELIAS. Is there a blanket around?

JIM. In there . . . (*Elias gets a blanket from the examining room. Headlights flash across the L. window.*)

ELIAS. What did I tell you? Here comes a car now. (*As Jim and Elias cover Doc, the headlights come to rest on the open front door, and are turned off. Simultaneously there is the sound of a car motor approaching and stopping, and then a car door slamming.*)

JIM. I have to go inside. Excuse me. (*He goes hurriedly out of sight R., leaving Elias looking after him. Bea enters L. distraught, her coat pulled on over a housecoat.*)

BEA. Zenia called me . . . (*She looks, then turns away with a hand to her eyes.*) oh God . . . (*Elias goes to her side and pats her shoulder, sighing and shaking his head.*) Where's Jim?

ELIAS. Inside. I think he's—being sick. Poor Helen near passed out when she heard.

BEA. Jim was going to check him over this very evening! That's why I wrote him, got him to come here . . . (*She cries. Elias gives her a handkerchief, she rubs at her eyes.*) thank you . . .

ELIAS. Listen, Bea; we've got to get Jim to stay. For a few weeks, at least. (*Blinking away tears, Bea looks at him.*) Shoreham lost their doctor last summer and they still haven't found a new one.

BEA. I asked him before, to come in with Doc, and he didn't want to. But now maybe he— (*She stops and they draw apart as Jim comes back into the examining room and out to join them. He has washed and freshened himself, and the effects of the poison are completely gone. He comes to Bea and puts a consoling hand*

55

on her shoulder. She looks up at him sadly.) it was—too late, wasn't it?

JIM. (*Nods.*) It happened quickly, though. I don't think he even had time to realize.

ELIAS. Will you write a certificate for me to give to Evalyn Ruth?

JIM. (*A pause.*) Of course I will.

ELIAS. Otherwise I'd have to call in the doctor from Davistown.

BEA. We were just saying that we hoped you'd stay on a while and look out for us here.

ELIAS. He hasn't got time for Greenfield, the doctor in Davistown.

JIM. I—I can't. I have to be in Chicago Tuesday morning. To see my draft board.

ELIAS. You stay put here, you'll be back under *our* draft board.

BEA. You said that your girl likes small-town living.

JIM. No. No, I—I don't want to be the only doctor, with nobody else to—share the load. (*The telephone rings.*) I'd like to help out, but I'm sorry, I can't.

BEA. (*Picking up the receiver.*) Yes?

ELIAS. You're not going to let us all down, are you, Jim?

JIM. Ah, don't put it that way, Elias. I know it's—   BEA. Oh, no! What was she doing there?

(*Jim and Elias turn to listen.*)

BEA. Oh my goodness! Of all nights . . . hold on a minute, Zenia. (*Covers the mouthpiece, looks at Jim.*) Peggy Scudder fell off of Patman's Rock. (*Jim and Elias wince and draw breath.*) They're afraid to move her; she's unconscious and bleeding from the mouth. (*A pause.*)

JIM. All right. I'll go. (*Goes L. into the foyer.*)

BEA. He's on his way, Zenia. Tell them he'll be there in ten minutes. (*Hangs up.*)

JIM. (*Getting his coat from the rack.*) Why the hell isn't there a higher fence up there?

ELIAS. Because Tom Lick won't have one. Doc warned him someone would fall but Tom is getting stubborner and stingier the older he gets! (*Getting into his coat in the foyer doorway, Jim freezes for a moment.*)

BEA. Take my car; it's blocking the driveway anyway.

JIM. (*Buttons his coat.*) I can probably postpone my meeting with the draft board for a day or two, long enough so that I can stay here for Doc's funeral. But that's as long as I'm *going* to stay. I don't want you to think I'm going to change my mind or stay on temporarily or anything. You'd better start right in looking for somebody else.

ELIAS. All right, Jim, we will. The first thing tomorrow morning. *(Bea takes Doc's bag from the desk and holds it out to Jim. He hesitates, then steps forward and takes it. He hefts the unfamiliar-familiar weight for a moment, and then, adjusted to it, goes determinedly from the house as the curtain falls.)*

END OF ACT THREE

THE END

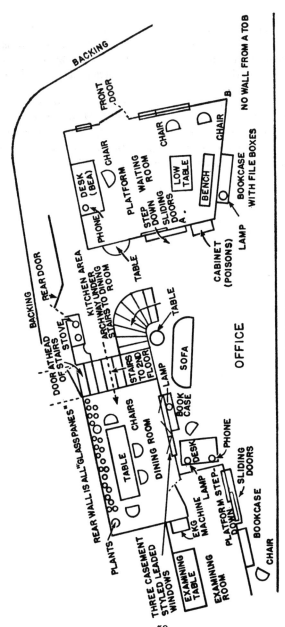

SCENE DESIGN

"DR. COOK'S GARDEN"

58

PROPERTY PLOT

Act I

OFFICE:
  Small chair, far R.
  Bookcase, R. of examining room door—

   On this bookcase:
   Assorted medical books, bric-a-brac, box files, accordion files
  Roll-top desk, L. of examining room door—

   On desk:
   Telephone, insurance form, 5x7 file cards, pads, pencils, papers,
   small potted plants, lamp, letter opener
  Swivel chair, at desk
  Bookcase, under dining room windows—

   On this bookcase:
   Medical books, box files, accordion files, small plants, lamp
  Framed cover of "Flower & Garden" magazine, on wall
  Small sofa, c.—

   On sofa:
   2 pillows
  Small table, above sofa
  Poison cabinet, beside waiting room door—

   In this cabinet:
   Bottles of pills, tablets, capsules, powders, crystals, etc., some
   with poison labels
  Bookcase, far L.—

   On this bookcase:
   5x7 file card boxes, small plants, accordion files, box files, lamp
  Rug, front of sofa
  Framed medical diplomas and certificates

EXAMINING ROOM:
  Examining table
  Electro-cardiograph machine
  Box-files on shelf above door
  X-ray pictures, in box files
  Blanket

DINING ROOM:
Table
4 chairs
2 brass candlesticks, on table

KITCHEN:
3 yellow mugs
Coffee pot
Tray
Assorted silverware
Assorted dishes
Tablecloth
Napkins
Shopping bag with knitting
Window shades

RECEPTION ROOM:
Desk—

On this desk:
Telephone, typewriter, assorted forms, pads, pencils, file cards
and boxes, envelopes for X-ray pictures
Metal ashstand
Desk chair
Coat rack
2 straight-backed chairs
Small coffee table—

On this table:
Assorted magazines

OFFSTAGE L.:
Man's two-suiter
Attaché case
Doctor's bag
Man's wallet with girl's photo (Jim)
Key ring and keys (one key for poison cabinet) (Doc)
Cigarettes
Matches
Fountain pen (Doc)

Act II

OFFICE:
Poison cabinet key, resting on top of *Flower and Gardens* frame
Strike: "Meserve" and "Maxim" cards to D. L. file box
No other changes

OFFICE:

Move coffee table from reception room to front of sofa

On coffee table:
Plate of beef stew, knife, fork, small bowl of salad, napkin, glass of wine

On roll-top desk:
Plate of beef stew, knife, fork, small bowl of salad, glass of wine, bottle of wine, napkin

EXAMINING ROOM:

On examining table:
White enamel basin containing rubber tubing, 2 hypo syringes, 6 ammonia ampules, small bottle of alcohol, cotton balls, plastic sheeting

RECEPTION ROOM:
Bolt front door

Off L.:
Pie plate, covered with napkin

NOTE: ELECTRIC PROPS

Practical lamps:
One each on roll-top desk, bookcase under dining room windows and bookcase D. L.

Simulated wall-switches:
One on office door-jamb, L.
One on wall close to kitchen

NOTE: PLANTS, FOLIAGE, GREENERY

Except for windows opening from office into dining room, all other windows have shelves holding small plants and seedlings. Hanging from ceiling of dining room are baskets of fern and ivy. Seen through the exterior dining room windows are trees, shrubbery, vines, etc.

COSTUME PLOT

Act I

DR. JIM TENNYSON:
Suit, medium brown
White shirt
Brown tie
Brown shoes
Brown socks
Light brown topcoat

BEA SCHMIDT:
White receptionist-nurse uniform
White shoes
White stockings
Grey tweed medium-weight outer coat
Handkerchief

DORA LUDLOW:
Blue-grey cotton blouse, white collar
Dark grey full skirt
White apron
Light beige stockings
Black shoes
Dark brown wool outer-coat
Handkerchief

ELIAS HART:
Dark plaid wool shirt
Dark brown corduroy trousers
Dark brown corduroy outer coat (loose fitting—car coat)
Brown shoes
Brown socks
Handkerchief

DR. LEONARD COOK:
Suit, grey
Black sweater-vest
White shirt, buttoned at collar—no tie
Black shoes
Black socks
"Car" or "suburban" coat, grey and black wool
Dark brown fedora hat

Act II

DR. TENNYSON:
Shirt, trousers, tie, shoes, socks—same as Act I

DR. COOK:
Same as Act I

Act III

DR. TENNYSON:
Only change—to white, short-sleeved sport shirt

DR. COOK:
Shirt, trousers, sweater-vest, shoes, socks—same as Acts I and II

ELIAS HART:
Except for outer coat, repeat Act I

BEA SCHMIDT:
Housedress, beige stockings, black shoes and repeat outer coat from Act I

NEW PLAYS

★ **MONTHS ON END by Craig Pospisil.** In comic scenes, one for each month of the year, we follow the intertwined worlds of a circle of friends and family whose lives are poised between happiness and heartbreak. "...a triumph...these twelve vignettes all form crucial pieces in the eternal puzzle known as human relationships, an area in which the playwright displays an assured knowledge that spans deep sorrow to unbounded happiness." *–Ann Arbor News.* "...rings with emotional truth, humor...[an] endearing contemplation on love...entertaining and satisfying." *–Oakland Press.* [5M, 5W] ISBN: 0-8222-1892-5

★ **GOOD THING by Jessica Goldberg.** Brings us into the households of John and Nancy Roy, forty-something high-school guidance counselors whose marriage has been increasingly on the rocks and Dean and Mary, recent graduates struggling to make their way in life. "...a blend of gritty social drama, poetic humor and unsubtle existential contemplation..." *–Variety.* [3M, 3W] ISBN: 0-8222-1869-0

★ **THE DEAD EYE BOY by Angus MacLachlan.** Having fallen in love at their Narcotics Anonymous meeting, Billy and Shirley-Diane are striving to overcome the past together. But their relationship is complicated by the presence of Sorin, Shirley-Diane's fourteen-year-old son, a damaged reminder of her dark past. "...a grim, insightful portrait of an unmoored family..." *–NY Times.* "MacLachlan's play isn't for the squeamish, but then, tragic stories delivered at such an unrelenting fever pitch rarely are." *–Variety.* [1M, 1W, 1 boy] ISBN: 0-8222-1844-5

★ **[SIC] by Melissa James Gibson.** In adjacent apartments three young, ambitious neighbors come together to discuss, flirt, argue, share their dreams and plan their futures with unequal degrees of deep hopefulness and abject despair. "A work...concerned with the sound and power of language..." *–NY Times.* "...a wonderfully original take on urban friendship and the comedy of manners—a *Design for Living* for our times..." *–NY Observer.* [3M, 2W] ISBN: 0-8222-1872-0

★ **LOOKING FOR NORMAL by Jane Anderson.** Roy and Irma's twenty-five-year marriage is thrown into turmoil when Roy confesses that he is actually a woman trapped in a man's body, forcing the couple to wrestle with the meaning of their marriage and the delicate dynamics of family. "Jane Anderson's bittersweet transgender domestic comedy-drama ...is thoughtful and touching and full of wit and wisdom. A real audience pleaser." *–Hollywood Reporter.* [5M, 4W] ISBN: 0-8222-1857-7

★ **ENDPAPERS by Thomas McCormack.** The regal Joshua Maynard, the old and ailing head of a mid-sized, family-owned book-publishing house in New York City, must name a successor. One faction in the house backs a smart, "pragmatic" manager, the other faction a smart, "sensitive" editor and both factions fear what the other's man could do to this house— and to them. "If Kaufman and Hart had undertaken a comedy about the publishing business, they might have written *Endpapers*...a breathlessly fast, funny, and thoughtful comedy ...keeps you amused, guessing, and often surprised...profound in its empathy for the paradoxes of human nature." *–NY Magazine.* [7M, 4W] ISBN: 0-8222-1908-5

★ **THE PAVILION by Craig Wright.** By turns poetic and comic, romantic and philosophical, this play asks old lovers to face the consequences of difficult choices made long ago. "The script's greatest strength lies in the genuineness of its feeling." *–Houston Chronicle.* "Wright's perceptive, gently witty writing makes this familiar situation fresh and thoroughly involving." *–Philadelphia Inquirer.* [2M, 1W (flexible casting)] ISBN: 0-8222-1898-4

DRAMATISTS PLAY SERVICE, INC.
440 Park Avenue South, New York, NY 10016 212-683-8960 Fax 212-213-1539
postmaster@dramatists.com www.dramatists.com

NEW PLAYS

★ **BE AGGRESSIVE by Annie Weisman.** Vista Del Sol is paradise, sandy beaches, avocado-lined streets. But for seventeen-year-old cheerleader Laura, everything changes when her mother is killed in a car crash, and she embarks on a journey to the Spirit Institute of the South where she can learn "cheer" with Bible belt intensity. "…filled with lingual gymnastics…stylized rapid-fire dialogue…" –*Variety*. "…a new, exciting, and unique voice in the American theatre…" –*BackStage West*. [1M, 4W, extras] ISBN: 0-8222-1894-1

★ **FOUR by Christopher Shinn.** Four people struggle desperately to connect in this quiet, sophisticated, moving drama. "…smart, broken-hearted…Mr. Shinn has a precocious and forgiving sense of how power shifts in the game of sexual pursuit. He promises to be a playwright to reckon with…" –*NY Times*. "A voice emerges from an American place. It's got humor, sadness and a fresh and touching rhythm that tell of the loneliness and secrets of life…[a] poetic, haunting play." –*NY Post*. [3M, 1W] ISBN: 0-8222-1850-X

★ **WONDER OF THE WORLD by David Lindsay-Abaire.** A madcap picaresque involving Niagara Falls, a lonely tour-boat captain, a pair of bickering private detectives and a husband's dirty little secret. "Exceedingly whimsical and playfully wicked. Winning and genial. A top-drawer production." –*NY Times*. "Full frontal lunacy is on display. A most assuredly fresh and hilarious tragicomedy of marital discord run amok…absolutely hysterical…" –*Variety*. [3M, 4W (doubling)] ISBN: 0-8222-1863-1

★ **QED by Peter Parnell.** Nobel Prize-winning physicist and all-around genius Richard Feynman holds forth with captivating wit and wisdom in this fascinating biographical play that originally starred Alan Alda. "QED is a seductive mix of science, human affections, moral courage, and comic eccentricity. It reflects on, among other things, death, the absence of God, travel to an unexplored country, the pleasures of drumming, and the need to know and understand." –*NY Magazine*. "Its rhythms correspond to the way that people—even geniuses—approach and avoid highly emotional issues, and it portrays Feynman with affection and awe." –*The New Yorker*. [1M, 1W] ISBN: 0-8222-1924-7

★ **UNWRAP YOUR CANDY by Doug Wright.** Alternately chilling and hilarious, this deliciously macabre collection of four bedtime tales for adults is guaranteed to keep you awake for nights on end. "Engaging and intellectually satisfying…a treat to watch." –*NY Times*. "Fiendishly clever. Mordantly funny and chilling. Doug Wright teases, freezes and zaps us." –*Village Voice*. "Four bite-size plays that bite back." –*Variety*. [flexible casting] ISBN: 0-8222-1871-2

★ **FURTHER THAN THE FURTHEST THING by Zinnie Harris.** On a remote island in the middle of the Atlantic secrets are buried. When the outside world comes calling, the islanders find their world blown apart from the inside as well as beyond. "Harris winningly produces an intimate and poetic, as well as political, family saga." –*Independent (London)*. "Harris' enthralling adventure of a play marks a departure from stale, well-furrowed theatrical terrain." –*Evening Standard (London)*. [3M, 2W] ISBN: 0-8222-1874-7

★ **THE DESIGNATED MOURNER by Wallace Shawn.** The story of three people living in a country where what sort of books people like to read and how they choose to amuse themselves becomes both firmly personal and unexpectedly entangled with questions of survival. "This is a playwright who does not just tell you what it is like to be arrested at night by goons or to fall morally apart and become an aimless yet weirdly contented ghost yourself. He has the originality to make you feel it." –*Times (London)*. "A fascinating play with beautiful passages of writing…" –*Variety*. [2M, 1W] ISBN: 0-8222-1848-8

DRAMATISTS PLAY SERVICE, INC.
440 Park Avenue South, New York, NY 10016 212-683-8960 Fax 212-213-1539
postmaster@dramatists.com www.dramatists.com

NEW PLAYS

★ SHEL'S SHORTS by Shel Silverstein. Lauded poet, songwriter and author of children's books, the incomparable Shel Silverstein's short plays are deeply infused with the same wicked sense of humor that made him famous. "...[a] childlike honesty and twisted sense of humor." —*Boston Herald.* "...terse dialogue and an absurdity laced with a tang of dread give [*Shel's Shorts*] more than a trace of Samuel Beckett's comic existentialism." —*Boston Phoenix.* [flexible casting] ISBN: 0-8222-1897-6

★ AN ADULT EVENING OF SHEL SILVERSTEIN by Shel Silverstein. Welcome to the darkly comic world of Shel Silverstein, a world where nothing is as it seems and where the most innocent conversation can turn menacing in an instant. These ten imaginative plays vary widely in content, but the style is unmistakable. "...[*An Adult Evening*] shows off Silverstein's virtuosic gift for wordplay...[and] sends the audience out...with a clear appreciation of human nature as perverse and laughable." —*NY Times.* [flexible casting] ISBN: 0-8222-1873-9

★ WHERE'S MY MONEY? by John Patrick Shanley. A caustic and sardonic vivisection of the institution of marriage, laced with the author's inimitable razor-sharp wit. "...Shanley's gift for acid-laced one-liners and emotionally tumescent exchanges is certainly potent..." —*Variety.* "...lively, smart, occasionally scary and rich in reverse wisdom." —*NY Times.* [3M, 3W] ISBN: 0-8222-1865-8

★ A FEW STOUT INDIVIDUALS by John Guare. A wonderfully screwy comedy-drama that figures Ulysses S. Grant in the throes of writing his memoirs, surrounded by a cast of fantastical characters, including the Emperor and Empress of Japan, the opera star Adelina Patti and Mark Twain. "Guare's smarts, passion and creativity skyrocket to awesome heights..." —*Star Ledger.* "...precisely the kind of good new play that you might call an everyday miracle...every minute of it is fresh and newly alive..." —*Village Voice.* [10M, 3W] ISBN: 0-8222-1907-7

★ BREATH, BOOM by Kia Corthron. A look at fourteen years in the life of Prix, a Bronx native, from her ruthless girl-gang leadership at sixteen through her coming to maturity at thirty. "...vivid world, believable and eye-opening, a place worthy of a dramatic visit, where no one would want to live but many have to." —*NY Times.* "...rich with humor, terse vernacular strength and gritty detail..." —*Variety.* [1M, 9W] ISBN: 0-8222-1849-6

★ THE LATE HENRY MOSS by Sam Shepard. Two antagonistic brothers, Ray and Earl, are brought together after their father, Henry Moss, is found dead in his seedy New Mexico home in this classic Shepard tale. "...His singular gift has been for building mysteries out of the ordinary ingredients of American family life..." —*NY Times.* "...rich moments ...Shepard finds gold." —*LA Times.* [7M, 1W] ISBN: 0-8222-1858-5

★ THE CARPETBAGGER'S CHILDREN by Horton Foote. One family's history spanning from the Civil War to WWII is recounted by three sisters in evocative, intertwining monologues. "...bittersweet music—[a] rhapsody of ambivalence...in its modest, garrulous way...theatrically daring." —*The New Yorker.* [3W] ISBN: 0-8222-1843-7

★ THE NINA VARIATIONS by Steven Dietz. In this funny, fierce and heartbreaking homage to *The Seagull,* Dietz puts Chekhov's star-crossed lovers in a room and doesn't let them out. "A perfect little jewel of a play..." —*Shepherdstown Chronicle.* "...a delightful revelation of a writer at play; and also an odd, haunting, moving theater piece of lingering beauty." —*Eastside Journal (Seattle).* [1M, 1W (flexible casting)] ISBN: 0-8222-1891-7

DRAMATISTS PLAY SERVICE, INC.
440 Park Avenue South, New York, NY 10016 212-683-8960 Fax 212-213-1539
postmaster@dramatists.com www.dramatists.com